L

3 4028 07972 3541
HARRIS COUNTY PUBLIC LIBRARY

D0850518

WITHDRAWN

Bloom's

GUIDES

Cormac McCarthy's
The Road

The Adventures of Huckleberry Finn
The Adventures of Tom Sawyer
All Quiet on the Western Front
Animal Farm
The Autobiography of Malcolm X
The Awakening
The Bell Jar
Beloved
Beowulf
Black Boy
The Bluest Eye
Brave New World
The Canterbury Tales
Catch-22
The Catcher in the Rye
The Chosen
A Christmas Carol
The Crucible
Cry, the Beloved Country
Death of a Salesman
Fahrenheit 451
A Farewell to Arms
Frankenstein
The Glass Menagerie
The Grapes of Wrath
Great Expectations
The Great Gatsby
The Handmaid's Tale
Heart of Darkness
The Hobbit
The House on Mango Street
I Know Why the Caged Bird Sings

The Iliad
Invisible Man
Jane Eyre
The Joy Luck Club
The Kite Runner
Lord of the Flies
Macbeth
Maggie: A Girl of the Streets
The Metamorphosis
Native Son
Night
1984
The Odyssey
Oedipus Rex
Of Mice and Men
One Hundred Years of Solitude
Pride and Prejudice
Ragtime
A Raisin in the Sun
The Red Badge of Courage
The Road
Romeo and Juliet
The Scarlet Letter
A Separate Peace
Slaughterhouse-Five
The Stranger
A Streetcar Named Desire
The Sun Also Rises
A Tale of Two Cities
Their Eyes Were Watching God
To Kill a Mockingbird
Uncle Tom's Cabin
The Waste Land
Wuthering Heights

Bloom's

GUIDES

Cormac McCarthy's
The Road

Edited & with an Introduction
by Harold Bloom

BLOOM'S
LITERARY CRITICISM
An Infobase Learning Company

Bloom's Guides: The Road
Copyright © 2011 by Infobase Learning
Introduction © 2011 by Harold Bloom

Bloom's Literary Criticism
An imprint of Infobase Learning
132 West 31st Street
New York, NY 10001

Library of Congress Cataloging-in-Publication Data
Cormac McCarthy's The road / edited and with an introduction by Harold Bloom.
    p. cm. — (Bloom's guides)
    Includes bibliographical references and index.
    ISBN 978-1-61753-002-9 (hardcover : alk. paper)
    1. McCarthy, Cormac, 1933– Road. 2. Fathers and sons in literature. 3. Good and evil in literature. 4. Apocalypse in literature. 5. Regression (Civilization) in literature. 6. Survival in literature. 7. Redemption in literature. I. Bloom, Harold. II. Title: Road.
    PS3563.C337R6333 2011
    813'.54—dc22
                                        2011000289

Contributing editor: Temple Cone
Cover designed by Takeshi Takahashi
Composition by IBT Global, Troy, NY
Cover printed by Yurchak Printing, Landisville, PA
Book printed and bound by Yurchak Printing, Landisville, PA
Date printed: June 2011
Printed in the United States of America
10 9 8 7 6 5 4 3 2 1

This book is printed on acid-free paper.

Contents

# Introduction

HAROLD BLOOM

Though I read Cormac McCarthy's first three novels with considerable interest, it was not until *Suttree* (1979) that he captured me. Six years later I was flooded by *Blood Meridian, or the Evening Redness in the West*. Only at the third attempt could I complete a first reading of that appalling masterwork, so overwhelmed was I by its violent power.

After many rereadings, I continue to be in awe of *Blood Meridian*. Three years older than McCarthy, I am his contemporary and view him from a different perspective than I do William Faulkner, Flannery O'Connor, and Carson McCullers. Like McCarthy, they are descendants of Herman Melville, whose *Moby-Dick* is the matrix from which *Blood Meridian* emerges.

After Faulkner, O'Connor, and McCullers (I would add Nathanael West), the major American fictions of our age seem to me *Blood Meridian*, Philip Roth's *Sabbath's Theater* and *American Pastoral*, Thomas Pynchon's several classics—*The Crying of Lot 49, Gravity's Rainbow, Mason & Dixon*—and Don DeLillo's *Underworld*.

After *Moby-Dick*, Melville never again achieved that eminence, except in shorter fictions. McCarthy's Border Trilogy and *No Country for Old Men* disappointed me, but *The Road* is difficult to judge. After a second reading I am puzzled by my experience of it and will need more time to see the book clearly.

Narratives set after apocalypse are a curious genre. McCarthy has the cunning not to give names either to the father or the son in *The Road*, thus recalling the nameless "kid" of *Blood Meridian*. Proper names do not work in a waste land. Personal identity there can be discovered only from within, as it were.

I could wish that either the father or his boy (of ten or eleven) had more touches of the individuality manifested by McCarthy's two protagonists in *Blood Meridian*, the quasi-Gnostic Archon or evil god of this world, Judge Holden, and "the kid" who slowly evolves into an unwilling moral heroism. In fairness to McCarthy, a cosmos that has suffered a global-warming catastrophe hardly allows for deep subjectivity in its survivors.

There seem to me two central questions for readers of *The Road* to confront. Is it a permanent literary achievement, and what precisely is its religious stance? I cannot at this time answer the first, because the book's pathos may not be fully earned, and yet that is perhaps an ungrateful response. Unlike *Blood Meridian*, where McCarthy brilliantly evades his own American Gnosticism, *The Road* shows elements of spiritual confusion. Ely is an unfortunate portrayal, unpersuasive and rather chaotic. Whether the father-son relationship avoids the abyss of sentimentality is also an equivocal matter.

McCarthy's audacity is admirable, and as a literary critic I affirm perpetual gratitude for *Blood Meridian*, which remains fresh and fierce after a quarter century. *The Road* probably will not sustain comparison to that greatness, but it merits careful rereading and pondering.

Biographical Sketch

Frequently proclaimed America's greatest living novelist, Cormac McCarthy has been likened to many of the great authors, including William Faulkner, for McCarthy's expansive and complex syntax and his attention to violence in southern society; Herman Melville, for McCarthy's obsessive attention to great spaces and his soaring metaphysical questions about the nature of God; Ernest Hemingway, for McCarthy's favoring of declarative sentences, his analysis of masculinity, and his interest in nature as a possible consolation in a violent world; and James Joyce, for the prismatic range of McCarthy's wordplay and his fervent attention to the workings of language and meaning. There are a range of other writers as well—including the Western genre writer Zane Grey, the southern gothic writers Carson McCullers and Flannery O'Connor, and the bleak existentialist Samuel Beckett—all of whom have contributed to the complex literary lineage of this novelist.

This detailed knowledge of McCarthy's literary ancestry contrasts with the relatively few known details about the life of this reticent and reclusive writer, at least in regard to his early years (McCarthy has given only a few interviews during his life and generally eschews the public eye). The eldest son and third of six children, Charles McCarthy was born on July 20, 1933, in Providence, Rhode Island; he later renamed himself Cormac after the ancient Irish king who built the Castle of Blarney. He grew up in Knoxville, Tennessee, where his family moved in 1937, and his first four novels take place in Tennessee, featuring rural southern landscapes (except for *Suttree*, which is set in Knoxville). An indifferent student, McCarthy attended the University of Tennessee from 1951–52, leaving to serve in the U.S. Air Force from 1953–56. He later returned to the University of Tennessee from 1957–60, completing several years of studies and receiving awards for his creative writing but ultimately leaving without a degree. In 1961, he married his first wife, Lee Holleman, and they moved to Chicago, where McCarthy worked as a mechanic and their son Cullen was born.

9

The marriage, however, did not last. In 1965, McCarthy divorced his wife, returned to Tennessee, and published his first novel, *The Orchard Keeper*, which was ushered through Random House by Albert Erskine, William Faulkner's longtime editor. The novel was praised for the simultaneous concreteness and metaphorical suggestiveness of its prose style, though some found it too heavily influenced by Faulkner. In the same year, on a traveling fellowship to Ireland from the American Academy of Arts and Letters, McCarthy met the singer Anne De Lisle, whom he married in 1966. From 1966 to 1968, McCarthy and De Lisle traveled the United Kingdom and France, often in the company of the novelist Leslie Garrett.

His 1968 novel, *Outer Dark*, was deemed more allegorical than his first, and it provoked a sharply divided response, with praise for its mix of vernacular and elevated styles and continued criticism for being derivative of the southern gothic tradition exemplified by writers such as Faulkner and Flannery O'Connor. Moving into a barn in Louisville, Tennessee, in 1969, McCarthy devoted the next few years to his novel *Suttree* and to a shorter book, *Child of God* (1974), which was based on an actual murder.

During these years when McCarthy's critical acclaim grew, he became increasingly private. In 1976, he left his wife and resettled in El Paso, Texas, a move that coincides with a dramatic shift in his writings. Though his next novel, *Suttree*, was published in 1979, after his move to Texas, it was a work 20 years in the making and is the last of McCarthy's books set in Tennessee. Though initial response was mixed, later critical and scholarly views hold that it is the pinnacle of his works about the region. After *Suttree*, however, McCarthy would take as his subject the history and legends of the American Southwest.

During the 1980s, McCarthy maintained a spartan lifestyle, living in rented rooms, operating on such a meager budget that one day, when he had used up his last bit of toothpaste and was too broke to afford more, a free sample arrived in the mail. During these years, he traveled frequently to Arizona, New

10

Mexico, and around Texas, researching the geography, layout, and history of those states for his new works.

In 1981, McCarthy received a so-called genius grant from the MacArthur Foundation and with the funds bought a stone cottage in El Paso. This new home afforded him the stability, the time, and the means to complete his next novel, arguably his greatest work and the one that has generated the richest critical and scholarly response, *Blood Meridian, Or the Evening Redness in the West*. The novel is a bleak, nihilistic account of a band of American scalp hunters on the Texas–Mexico border in the 1840s, and the richness of its languages, its allusions, and its meditations on violence and death have led critic Harold Bloom to claim that McCarthy "has attained genius with that book."

During the 1980s, McCarthy worked on *The Stonemason*, a play that was not published until 1994. Seven years passed before his next novel, *All the Pretty Horses*, which brought McCarthy a measure of popular success to match the praise he had been accorded by academics and distinguished critics. The first novel in what would be called the Border Trilogy, *All the Pretty Horses* follows the journey of 16-year-old John Grady Cole from Texas into Mexico, where he becomes a horse trainer, survives a Mexican prison, and pursues a doomed love affair with the daughter of a Mexican hacendado. The novel won a National Book Award and a National Book Critics Circle Award, and it was made into a feature film.

In 1994, McCarthy published *The Crossing*, the second novel of the Border Trilogy, which introduces the character Billy Parham. Then in 1998 he completed the trilogy with *Cities of the Plain*, which brings Cole and Parham together and depicts their efforts to maintain their old western virtues of courage, honesty, and loyalty in the face of the changing world of the early 1950s. In 1998, McCarthy married his current wife, Jennifer Winkley, and they later moved to Santa Fe, New Mexico, where McCarthy became involved with the Santa Fe Institute, a nonprofit organization devoted to scientific research. In 1998 the couple had a son, John, whom McCarthy claims is the basis for the unnamed boy in *The Road*.

With the *Border Trilogy* completed, McCarthy began setting his works closer to the present. In *No Country for Old Men* (2005), he keeps the setting in the Southwest but follows the violent aftermath of a failed drug deal in 1980. With *The Road* (2006), McCarthy propels his viewers into a dystopic vision of the future. For his efforts, he was awarded the Pulitzer Prize for Fiction the following year.

The Story Behind the Story

The Road is Cormac McCarthy's tenth novel and, in its depiction of a postapocalyptic future, it is perhaps his darkest. While McCarthy's earlier novels deal explicitly with violence, murder, torture, rape, and incest, *The Road* surpasses them in its almost absolute atmosphere of meaninglessness and menace. As author Michael Chabon notes in his review of the novel, "The eventual safety of a character in a McCarthy novel is always in doubt, but the reader's usual sense that a disembowelment or a clean shot to the brainpan lies only a paragraph away has never been so excruciating as in *The Road*, where the life of a child whose innocence is literally singular is threatened from the first paragraph of the novel" (112).

The mood of heightened anxiety that McCarthy creates, which Chabon associates with the tradition of gothic and horror literature (116), is matched by counterbalancing tones of hope and redemption. With each of these modes, it is the relation between the unnamed father and son that generates the novel's visceral emotional intensity, a quality praised by a range of critics and commentators. Scholar Thomas Schaub describes the novel as a profound spiritual journey, one that locates "the basis for meaning in [a] father's love for his son" (Schaub 153).

The father-son bond, with all its worries, demands, and challenges, is not only at the thematic heart of the novel but also at the heart of the work's creation. McCarthy, who was 75 at the time of the novel's publication, is the father of two sons, one of whom, John, was 11 when the novel was published. In a *Wall Street Journal* interview, McCarthy claims that much of the material for the story came from conversations he had with John, to whom the book is dedicated. Thus, much of the anxiety the unnamed father in *The Road* feels about the uncertain and violent future his son faces is paralleled by McCarthy's own anxieties as a father well past middle age, worried about the future his son will face possibly without him. As Chabon observes, "*The Road* is not a record of fatherly fidelity; it is a testament to the abyss of a parent's greatest fears," including the fear of dying before the child has grown to adulthood and of leaving the child a world "more damaged, more poisoned, more base and violent and cheerless and toxic, more doomed, than the one you inherited" (120). McCarthy himself remarks that "[y]our future gets shorter and you recognize that. In recent years, I have had no desire to do anything but work and be with John" (WSJ 1). McCarthy conveys this fear of loss and its opposing dedication to what remains throughout the novel; in one instance, while watching his son asleep by a fire, the father begins weeping: "He wasn't sure what it was about but he thought it was about beauty or about goodness" (109).

Yet for all the fear and worry the novel conveys, it also depicts the hope and redemptive love that can come from this bond, an intense, self-sacrificing love that is at times unreservedly religious and transcendent in tone. Behind the intense love that the unnamed man in *The Road* feels for his son, whom the man calls "a god" (145), are McCarthy's own feelings for his son. "(P)eople tell me from time to time that my son John is just a wonderful kid," he tells *The Wall Street Journal*. "I tell people that he is so morally superior to me that I feel foolish correcting him about things" (1). This desire to protect and nourish goodness in the face of violence and cruelty, forces that McCarthy explores in depth and with chilling insight in his earlier novels, drives both the unnamed father and McCarthy himself to tell "old stories of courage and justice" (35), and in their telling, to find the strength to live out such stories themselves. "I don't think goodness is something that you learn," claims McCarthy. "If you're left adrift in the world to learn goodness from it, you would be in trouble. . . . There's not much you can do to try to make a child into something that he's not. But whatever he is, you can sure destroy it. Just be mean and cruel and you can destroy the best person" (1). Such musings inform the world of *The Road*, in which fundamental moral struggles are played out on a bleak stage of a barren postapocalyptic landscape.

List of Characters

The unnamed man (also called Papa by his son) is the protagonist of the novel. His thoughts, emotions, and memories are articulated by a narrator who often seems identical with or a double of the man (though, in fact, the novel continues after the man dies). A survivor of the apocalypse that has turned the United States into a sunless, ashen landscape populated by nomadic scavengers and by tribes of cannibals, he is utterly devoted to his son, whom he considers "his warrant" (4), "the word of God" (4), and even a god (145). McCarthy reveals little of the father's life before the event that destroyed the natural world. When the man and his son visit the ruined house where the man grew up, McCarthy reveals that the man had sisters (22); at another point, a cannibal who stumbles upon the father and son asks, "'Are you a doctor?'" (55) after the father threatens to shoot him, saying the bullet "will be in your brain before you can hear it. To hear it you will need a frontal lobe and things with names like colliculus and temporal gyrus and you wont have them anymore" (55). Most important, in terms of the man's past, is that he was once married, and his wife killed herself a few years earlier after "the hundred nights they'd sat up debating the pros and cons of self destruction with the earnestness of philosophers chained to a madhouse wall" (49). As the novel progresses, the man gradually succeeds in making himself forget that past life, even discarding the last photo he possesses of his wife, so that he can face the horrors of the present, since "the right dreams for a man in peril were dreams of peril and all else was the call of languor and of death" (15). The man is skilled at surviving in the ravaged world, which entails scavenging for supplies, hiding, fighting when necessary, tinkering with mechanical devices, and navigating a landscape altered by deforestation, fires, and decay.

The unnamed boy is the son of the unnamed man and is the other central character in the novel. Born a few days after the mysterious apocalypse, his age is unspecified, though it appears he is between the ages of 8 and 11, with most readers identifying him as 10; at one point, the father carries him on his shoulders (56); the son also struggles for independence, as when he quarrels with his father about whether or not to go looking for a little boy he claims to have seen (72). His only knowledge of the world is of its ruined state, and he relates to his father at times as if the latter were "an alien. A being from a planet that no longer existed. The tales of which were suspect" (129). Over the course of the novel, both the boy and his father come to see that he is "the one" on whom the future depends, because he must learn to be moral in this ruined world without ever having lived in the paradise of the past. As a result, the boy grows from a child's complete and loving dependence on his father to an imperfect but more understanding and ultimately compassionate bond.

The unnamed woman (also referred to as "the wife" or "the mother") committed suicide several years before the start of the novel. McCarthy reveals even less about her past than about the father's, noting only that she and the man had a physical relationship, that she was pregnant at the time of the cataclysmic event, and that she gave birth to the boy a few days later. Though she lived with the man and the boy for some time after the catastrophe, at one point she decides that she cannot continue to endure the world in its present state, warning the man that "Sooner or later [the cannibals] will catch us and they will kill us. They will rape me. They'll rape him. They are going to rape us and kill us and eat us" (48). Yet her suicide is a strangely selfless act, since "the coldness of [her departure] was her final gift," helping the man sever his emotional ties to her so that he might attend more fully to the boy.

Ely is a nearly blind wanderer whom the man and the boy encounter after they have left the safety of the fallout shelter. He is a prophetic figure, whose blindness seems to enable a higher vision, though not the accompanying power to affect the future. As he says, "People were always getting ready for tomorrow. I didnt believe in that. Tomorrow wasnt getting ready for them. It didnt even know they were there" (142). He is the only character in the novel with a name, much less one with great allegorical significance. In the biblical book of Kings, the prophet Elijah brings down fire from the sky and mounts to heaven in a whirlwind; elsewhere Jesus is compared to him, giving the postapocalyptic setting of *The Road* resonance with the Last Judgment. After spending a night with the man and the boy, Ely disappears the next day, "dwindling slowly on the road behind them like some storybook peddler from an antique time, dark and bent and spider thin and soon to vanish forever" (147).

The man struck by lightning is the first living person McCarthy presents after introducing the man and his son. Though only briefly presented, he seems to symbolize the world in its postapocalyptic state: stunned, disordered, and dying. The father's words to his son—"We cant help him. There's nothing to be done for him" (43)—offer bleak commentary on the possibility that the world might recover from its ruin.

The cannibal whom the father shoots is representative of the other cannibals in the novel, who make "reptilian calculations" (64) and would "eat your children in front of your eyes" (152). The narrator states that the cannibal's violation of a taboo against eating human flesh has uprooted all morality and "has made of the world a lie every word" (64). Defending his son from the cannibal's knife, the man shoots him with one of his two remaining bullets, meaning that in the future, only he or his son will have the option of suicide in the face of capture and slow death.

The thief who steals all the possessions of the man and boy after the boy recovers from his illness is an "outcast from one of the communes" (215), his mutilated right hand a mark of Cain indicating his status as a pariah. In anger at his theft, the man takes all of the thief's clothes from him at gunpoint and sends him naked into the dark; this violation of the rule of the "good guys" horrifies the boy and forces him to realize that his father is not a hero but a flawed man trying to make his way in a fallen world.

The **"veteran of old skirmishes" (237)** and **his wife** appear only at the end of the novel. Well-equipped and with two children, they have been following the man and the boy, and though the veteran is a bit puzzled by the boy's talk about "good guys" and "the fire," he and his wife take the boy into their family after the father dies.

Summary and Analysis

Cormac McCarthy's novel *The Road* takes place in the southern United States in the near future, approximately ten years after an unidentified global catastrophe caused widespread fires and clouded the upper atmosphere, resulting in the extinction of most life and the collapse of human civilization. In this new world, the few remaining people survive in settlements (none of which McCarthy depicts), as roving tribes surviving by cannibalism, or as solitary wanderers scavenging from the ruined land. The novel follows two scavengers, an unnamed father and son, during their long journey south toward the gulf coast to escape the impending winter and a vague but looming threat of increased violence coming from the north. At its core, the novel is concerned with how one creates and clings to meaning in a world of darkness and disorder; in this case, that meaning is linked to the sacrament of a father's enduring love for his son.

Readers encountering Cormac McCarthy for the first time may be challenged by many elements of his writing, most notably his style. McCarthy has long been known for stripping his writing of most of the formal punctuation that modern readers expect. He writes dialogue without quotation marks and often without attributions (the "he said"/ "she said" common to most fiction), which can confuse the reader but which can also create a sort of choral effect, so that it seems as if what one character says could just as easily be said by another. McCarthy drops the apostrophe in many contractions (preferring "dont" instead of "don't," for example), perhaps to convey by means of the text the gritty and blunt speech patterns of his characters, many of whom come from the working class. McCarthy is also a master of the sentence fragment, a grammatical construction in which the subject or main verb of the sentence is missing; for instance, after writing of how "The land was gullied and eroded and barren" (149), he manifests that erosion in a series of sentence fragments, writing of "[t]he bones of dead creatures sprawled in the washes. Middens of anonymous trash. Farmhouses in the fields scoured of their paint and the clapboards spooned and sprung from the wallstuds. All of it shadowless and without future" (149–50). According to one review of *The Road*, "McCarthy's fragmented style throughout suggests that human speech and human narrative must also—like other primitive skills—be reconstituted [in the wake of the apocalypse]" (Shy 39).

Yet for all the challenges that McCarthy's stylistic innovations present the reader, several have particular thematic resonance in *The Road*. McCarthy habitually blocks off individual paragraphs, rather than running them together as continuous text with indentations to indicate paragraph breaks, thus making each paragraph appear complete and distinct from the others, almost as if it were a prose poem. This visual device emphasizes the separateness or the division between the events and meditations in each paragraph, suggesting that in a ruined future such as the one McCarthy portrays, every moment of the present is distinct, set apart from the others, and worthy of the attention one must give to a lyric poem. To view this device another way, on a practical level, in the dangerous world McCarthy depicts, one must be forever alert to one's surroundings or face potentially fatal consequences. It is also the case, though, that in such a ruined world, where the past is irrelevant and the future without promise, the present moment is the only reality, as the concern the boy shows his ailing father demonstrates: "The boy watched him. In some other world the child would already have begun to vacate him from his life. But he had no life other. He knew the boy lay awake in the night and listened to hear if he were breathing" (229–30).

More important is McCarthy's distinct blend of vernacular speech patterns with the poetic diction of his narrative voice, which draws on a range of uncommon and archaic words, often with specifically religious connotations (for example, *firedrake, ensepulchred, tabernacle, salitter*). As a result of this wide lexical range, McCarthy creates what the Russian formalist critic Viktor Shklovsky calls "defamiliarization," a reinvigoration of language transforming its customary, often conventional usage by means of new and strange stylistic patterns. Defamiliarization makes readers aware of how words refer to things in the world; how words bear multiple, even contradictory meanings; and how ambiguities, sometimes confusing, sometimes meaningful, can arise between words and their references. This stylistic quality is correlated to one of the novel's major thematic concerns: the problem of the loss of meaning when much of the world to which language refers has been obliterated by the apocalypse, "uncoupled from its shoring" (10). As McCarthy puts it: "The world [was] shrinking down about a raw core of parsible entities. The names of things slowly following those things into oblivion. Colors. The names of birds. Things to eat. Finally the names of things one believed to be true. More fragile than he would have thought. How much was gone already? The sacred idiom shorn of its referents and so of its reality" (75).

Scholars debate about the thematic implications of defamiliarization in *The Road*, particularly the religious implications. Michael Chabon views it affirmatively, if unintentionally so; for him, the novel illustrates "(t)he paradox of language undoing the death it deals [in] every passage of the novel . . . evoking even as it denies" (114). But according to Shelly L. Rambo, the novel depicts a world in "the moments after the collapse of redemption" (107); therefore, it is appropriate that the language of redemption that McCarthy deploys throughout "is exposed, not in order to reveal its violence or to claim its fulfillment, but as a remnant of an irrecoverable world" (101). Thus, although the novel may seem nihilistic and despairing in its bleakness, such despair is "an imperative to witness to what remains when all constructs for meaning have been shattered" (114), driving the reader to consider, without the wish-fulfilling promise of rescue and redemption, how the world is ordered and made meaningful and how those ways of making meaning are now being destroyed. Thomas A. Carlson finds that the defamiliarization of the novel operates at the level of plot and character, as well as in language, and he views the resulting disorientation positively. He remarks that the loss and peril faced by the characters in *The Road* confront them "if only through an absence or failure, with the barest essential conditions of their worldly life and its possibility—conditions now illuminated by their very darkening" (54). Thus, the reader sees the world "in its essential vulnerability" and thus with new eyes, realizing that "it well could have not been, and could yet cease to be" (59).

McCarthy achieves a similar effect with his characters' names, or lack thereof. All but one of the characters in the novel are unnamed, as if, in the wake of the catastrophe that ruined the world, all past identities have been erased. The one character McCarthy names is Ely, an old man whose name refers to the biblical prophet Elijah, a figure likened to John the Baptist and Jesus Christ, who raises the dead, summons fire from the heavens, and finally ascends to heaven in a whirlwind. This allusion has led scholar Carl James Grindley to view the setting of *The Road* as a post-Revelation landscape, the world that remains after the blessed souls have ascended to heaven in rapture and God's final judgment has brought hellish torment to the damned (12–13). At the very least, the anonymity of the characters suggests the loss of individual personality that seems to follow death, and indeed, the novel is populated by figures who seem more dead than alive. At one point, the father discards the contents of his wallet—"Some money, credit cards. His driver's license. A picture of his wife" (43)—a gesture signaling the loss of conventionally modern ways of defining oneself (through economic, social, or marital status). The one exception to this loss of identity is the man's role as a father; "(h)e knew only that the child was his warrant" (4), McCarthy writes, suggesting that the man's sole reason for existence is to serve as father to his son, a sacred duty that earns him the name by which the boy calls him, "Papa."

One final feature of McCarthy's style that both complicates and enriches the text is its dense use of allusion. Along with the biblical references to the prophet Elijah and to Revelation, the novel is filled with references to major literary works, especially the *Divine Comedy* of Dante; T. S. Eliot's poem *The Waste Land*; Ernest Hemingway's short story collection *In Our Time*, particularly the two-part short story "Big Two-Hearted River"; and W.B. Yeats's poem "The Second Coming." While it is not necessary to have read these works to appreciate the novel, one gains immeasurably from understanding the thematic and imagistic links between the novel and these other works. Just as the burned-out landscapes depicted by Eliot and Hemingway evoke the literal and psychological damage of World War I, so McCarthy's "cauterized terrain" (12) suggests the ravages of nuclear holocaust or of global climate change. The monster that the father dreams of in the opening pages of the novel resembles the "rough beast / slouch[ing] towards Bethlehem" in Yeats's poem "The Second Coming," a work often read as both a prediction of and political commentary on the violence of the twentieth century. The journey of the man and boy through a hellish landscape toward some promise of salvation mirrors the journey taken by the poet Dante and the ghost of the Roman poet Virgil in Dante's epic poem *The Divine Comedy*.

Yet McCarthy does not simply allude to these texts; his references sometimes function in inverse fashion. While Eliot could claim at the end of *The Waste Land* to have "shored these fragments" of culture and art "against my ruins," achieving some measure of order in a world radically altered by World War I, McCarthy writes of how meaning itself has come "uncoupled from its shoring" (10) in the wake of environmental disaster. If Yeats's rough beast "slouches toward Bethlehem," threatening to drown "the ceremony of innocence," then McCarthy's beast "lurche[s] away" (4) from a world that has already been destroyed. And while Virgil and Dante escape the Inferno and Dante ascends into the heavenly Paradise, the boy will remain in the hellish world of *The Road* even after his father's death, albeit with a new family to protect him.

In contrast to these complexities of style and allusion, the plot of *The Road* is relatively simple. It follows the journey of the unnamed father and son as they push a shopping cart loaded with their worldly goods along a succession of roads southward in order to escape the coming winter and a looming threat the father fears from the north. It is a world that has suffered not only a global environmental catastrophe, but a profound moral and human one as well:

The world [was] largely populated by men who would eat your children in front of your eyes and the cities themselves were held by cores of blackened looters who tunneled among the ruins and crawled from the rubble white of tooth and eye carrying charred and anonymous tins of food in nylon nets like shoppers in the commissaries of hell. The soft black talc blew through the streets like squid ink uncoiling along a sea floor and the cold crept down and the dark came early . . . (152–53)

Michael Chabon finds in the novel elements of postapocalyptic science fiction, the modern adventure story, the epic (particularly the traditional descent of the hero into the realms of the dead), and gothic horror. According to scholar Thomas H. Schaub, the novel follows the structure of a traditional spiritual journey concerned with the experience "of losing one's way in the middle of life, of things falling apart, of life as a wasteland, of having lost Paradise" (154), though the end points of those traditional journeys—Jerusalem, Canterbury, the recovery of the Holy Grail, Paradise itself—appear to be missing in McCarthy's "barren, silent, godless" landscape (*Road* 4). Woven throughout the events of this journey are numerous passages addressing the important philosophical questions the book raises, often articulated by an anonymous narrator who, while not the man himself, is omnisciently privy to his thoughts.

The novel opens with the protagonist, an unnamed man, waking from a dream and reaching out in the dark to touch his sleeping son: "When he woke in the woods in the dark and the cold of the night he'd reach out to touch the child sleeping beside him. Nights dark beyond darkness and the days more gray each one than what had gone before. Like the onset of some cold glaucoma dimming away the world. His hand rose and fell softly with each precious breath" (3). The opening sentences introduce some of the novel's principal themes: the conflict between darkness, cold, and blindness in the postapocalyptic world with human touch and intimacy, the innocence of childhood, and the preciousness of life itself. In addition, the opening statements refer to two of the most important works of Western literature: the *Republic* of Plato and *The Divine Comedy* of Dante. The dream from which the man wakes resembles the Allegory of the Cave that Plato describes in the *Republic*, in which the commonplace experience of reality is compared to the experience of watching shadows on a cave wall, while the truth is the experience of stepping forth into the sunlight, which is painful at first, then purifying. In the world of *The Road*, the absence of direct sunlight as a result of the great environmental disaster seems to have precluded access to the truth, which Plato often refers to as "the Good." The dark woods in which the main character finds himself recall the dark woods in which Dante is lost at the start of the *Inferno*: "Midway on our life's journey, I found myself / In dark woods, the right road lost" (I. 1–2).

The first section of the novel introduces the ruined landscape, the man and his son, and details about the man's past life, culminating in an encounter with one of the "bloodcults," the roving gangs of cannibals that terrify the father. Ash and dead trees dominate the landscape, and along with the profound darkness, they signify the disaster the world has suffered. Standing in contrast to this background of waste and deprivation is the father's utter commitment to his son, McCarthy's way of introducing the dual themes of faith lost and faith reclaimed by love: "He knew only that the child was his warrant. He said: If he is not the word of God God never spoke" (4). As the man makes breakfast, a description of his pistol is offered, its early appearance underscoring its great importance in their lives, not so much as a weapon of defense, since the pistol only holds two bullets, but, as McCarthy later reveals, as a means of suicide.

The first words the man and boy speak to each other prove emblematic of their characters throughout the novel, just as the opening sentences of the book reveal its key themes and characteristic style. The boy's first words to his father upon waking, "Hi, Papa," reveal not only the boyish innocence that he will demonstrate throughout the novel but also shows the utter importance of his father in his life, since he is the first thing the boy mentions upon waking. The father's reply, "I'm right here," and the boy's answer, "I know" (5), show not only the father's utmost devotion to his child and his resolve always to be with him but also the boy's faith and confidence that his father will be present. Read closely, this dialogue shows McCarthy establishing a connection between father and son that resonates with the Christian notion of the bond between God the Father and Jesus, a point McCarthy emphasizes when he writes that they were "each the other's world entire" (5).

Traveling by day and camping at night, the man and boy live out what would seem an ordinary, albeit impoverished, life, but for the dangerous and extreme circumstances in which they find themselves. In many ways, the setting of *The Road* intensifies ordinary facts of life that many people take for granted, so that routine occurrences, especially in a child's life, take on an almost existential importance. For instance, the father worries "mostly . . . about their shoes. That and food. Always food" (15), the repetition emphasizing the centrality of this concern. One night, after looking out over a ruined city before bedding down, the boy asks for the light until he is asleep (8), a costly request given the scarcity of fuel but one that illuminates how disorienting and terrifying the dark can be. At another point, the boy asks the father questions about death, notably "What would you do if I died?" (9), a question McCarthy claims his own young son John has asked him (Jurgensen 1). The father replies that he would want to die too, "So I could be with you" (9), a feeling shared by many parents for their children but one brought to the fore by this dangerous world. The man's honesty contrasts with the loss of meaning evident almost everywhere else; the narrator notes that even "the sacred idiom [is] shorn of its referents and so of its reality" (75), and the father wishes, "If only my heart were stone" (10). He suffers in this world precisely because he clings to the old meanings of words, those that refer to the material objects of this world and also those that refer to the abstract virtues.

Throughout this first section of the book, McCarthy provides memories of the father's past life, often to provide a shocking juxtaposition with the world in its current condition. For instance, the man remembers fishing on the lake at his father's farm, realizing that "This was the perfect day of his childhood. This the day to shape the days upon" (12), an observation shortly followed by a description of the land as a "cauterized terrain" (12) and an "ashen scabland" (13). When the man and boy stop to scavenge at an old gas station, the man tries dialing his own father's former phone number, prompting the boy to ask what he is doing (6), since the child was born after the world's catastrophe and has never known the unblighted world the man (and by extension, the reader) once knew, in which technology worked and society was civil.

Most of the man's memories are of his dead wife. The first time she is mentioned, she appears to him in a dream strangely dressed and with her ribs painted white (15), a spectral figure of death itself. According to McCarthy, "He mistrusted all of that. He said the right dreams for a man in peril were dreams of peril and all else was the call of languor of death" (15). Yet he also wishes to hold onto the memories, in defiance of his own injunction to survive: "Freeze this frame," he thinks. "Now call down your dark and your cold and be damned" (16). The reader learns that the wife was pregnant when the apocalypse occurred (41), delivered the boy a few days later (50), and lived with the two of them a number of years before deciding to kill herself. Her final conversation with her husband is a poignant moment in the book, for her decision seems both an act of despair and a profound act of self-sacrifice. She knows that they only have bullets enough for two of them to commit suicide in the event that they are captured; she believes that their capture, rape, death, and consumption by cannibals are only a matter of time; and she knows that her husband will not give up his doomed effort to survive. She wants to take her son's life as well, to spare him future suffering, but she knows "you wont survive for yourself. I know because I would never have come this far" (49). When she departs, she does so brusquely, to help her husband sever his emotional ties with her and move beyond grief and to face the reality before him. In a sense, she gives up her life and her bond to her son so that they might live: "A person who had no one would be well advised to cobble together some passable ghost," she warns. "Breathe it into being and coax it along with words of love. Offer it each phantom crumb and shield if from harm with your body" (49).

For scholar Thomas H. Schaub, McCarthy's narration of forgotten memories, which subsequently revives their presence on the page, is a characteristic device in the novel (155), and he associates it with a peculiar feature of McCarthy's syntax, in which he "purposely holds out first the image of life and then its ashen reality" (157). The man experiences, for instance, "the uncanny taste of a peach from some phantom orchard fading in his mouth" (16), while at another time, the narrator describes how "(t)he country went from pine to liveoak and pine. Magnolias," calling to mind the forests of the American Southeast, only to observe that they were "(t)rees as dead as any" (165). Such frequent transitions in image, from a living memory to the dead present, not only elicit sympathy from the reader but also reenact the recurring fall of the world into ruin. In a sense, McCarthy's syntactical device enacts the memory of trauma; as the father describes it, "You forget what you want to remember and you remember what you want to forget" (10).

During this first section of the novel, the man and boy travel and scavenge, visiting the home the man grew up in (21–23), experiencing an earthquake (23–24), hearing dead trees fall at night (30), and camping beside a waterfall, where they go swimming and eat a meal of dried morels (31–35), prompting the boy to say, "This is a good place Papa" (35). The bodies of water they encounter are devoid of life, an ironic refutation of the romantic ideal of nature as a source of generative power and rejuvenation, as McCarthy demonstrates in a scene that evokes Hemingway's short story "Big Two-Hearted River, Part One." In Hemingway's story, the wounded World War I veteran Nick Adams looks down at trout in a river and associates their ability to hold steady in the current with the possibility that he will be able to recover from his psychological traumas. In *The Road*, the father notes that "He'd stood at such a river once and watched the flash of trout deep in a pool, invisible to see in the teacolored water except as they turned on their sides to feed" (35), but the flash of both trout and insight is absent from this scene, suggesting that one of the great losses in this new world is nature's healing force.

After crossing a bridge blocked by a jackknifed truck, the trailer of which the man inspects and finds filled with mummified bodies (40), the father and son encounter a man who has been struck by lightning. The boy, clearly wishing for companionship in this lonely world, asks to help the man, but the father's reply—"There's nothing to be done for him" (43)—not only ends the conversation but serves as a poignant comment on the state of the world, which can no longer be helped, having been struck and all but destroyed by an event as unpredictable and intensely powerful as a lightning strike. After discarding the last photo of his wife in his possession and remembering vividly his final conversations with her, the man wakes one morning to see a group of strangely and menacingly clad figures approaching on the road, their image evoking the "rough beast" from Yeats's poem "The Second Coming": "They came shuffling through the ash casting their hooded heads from side to side. Some of them wearing canister masks. One in a biohazard suit. Stained and filthy. Slouching along with clubs in their hands, lengths of pipe. Coughing" (50). They are members of one of the *bloodcults*, the word combining elements of violence and crazed worship. Fearing for their safety, the man wakes his son, and together they dash into the woods, leaving behind the shopping cart that holds most of their possessions. Watching from the woods, the father sees that the bloodcult members have been traveling in a diesel truck, which has stalled. While repairs are being made, a man walks into the woods to relieve himself.

The encounter with the man is a crucial episode in the book. For one, he is the first cannibal McCarthy depicts close up, and his description, "(l)ike an animal inside a skull looking out the eyeholes" (53), reveals the bestial depths to which this individual and his ilk have sunk. "What are you eating," the father asks him; "Whatever we can find," the man answers ominously (54). His attempt to lure the father and son with an offer of food demonstrates the breakdown in personal exchanges in this world, revealing that the father's fears and paranoia are in fact well-founded and that the cannibal's existence and the threat he represents have "made of the world a lie every word" (64). When the cannibal grabs the boy and holds a knife to his throat, the father's decision to shoot the man in the head costs him one of their two remaining bullets and thus the means of escaping the misery and menace of the present through suicide.

The killing also shows the lengths to which the father will go to protect and preserve his son, and McCarthy suggests that both the killing and its aftermath are events that bear religious significance. After they have escaped their pursuers and the father has washed gore from the boy's hair in a scene "like some ancient anointing," the man tells himself, "This is my child. . . . I wash a dead man's brains out of his hair. That is my job" (63). Stroking his son's "pale and tangled hair" as he sleeps, the father realizes the boy is a "[g]olden chalice, good to house a god" (64), and this realization provides the man a sense of mission sealed in the pair's shared blood: "My job is to take care of you," he tells his son. "I was appointed to do that by God. I will kill anyone who touches you" (65). Yet it is a mission darkened by the understanding that, as a father, he might be forced to kill his son to save him from the evils of the world and that that consolation may not be available to him either: "A single round left in the revolver. You will face the truth. You will not" (58).

Ironically, the boy often finds his role in the relationship altered and intensified by the present circumstances. The son motivates his father to perform some of the actions of parenthood common to life before the apocalypse, such as reading him a bedtime story (7) or teaching him to swim (33), in spite of the despair the man might feel at the uselessness of such activities in a ruined world. The son also turns to the father for moral assurance, as when the adult tells the child that they would not eat the dog they hear barking one night (69–70), or later, when the man assures the boy that they would never eat a person, no matter how hungry they became (108–09). The boy must also, in a sense, be a parent to his father, preventing him from sacrificing himself for his son in a propitiatory way, as when the boy makes the father share a Coca Cola with him instead of drinking it all himself, or when, catching his father giving the boy the entire amount of cocoa instead of splitting it, he reminds him that "You promised not to do that," saying "If you break little promises you'll break big ones. That's what you said" (29). The preservation of such bonds through the practice of small, routine acts, a practice that could be described as sacramental, is crucial in a world in which such acts and attitudes could easily be overlooked and forgotten; as the narrator observes: "The last instance of a thing takes the class with it" (24). If the father stops acting like a father or the son like a son, then in a sense, those bonds and defined roles will be forever lost.

After hiding out for a night, the father and his son return to where they encountered the cannibals, and the father finds the slain man has been butchered and eaten by his companions. They recover the few possessions the cannibals did not take and begin their journey again. Along the way, the boy plays a flute the man carves from a piece of cane, "a formless music for the age to come. Or perhaps the last music on earth called up from out of the ashes of its ruin" (66), the ambivalent representation of the music again characteristic of McCarthy's artful syntax, which evokes a presence only to emphasize its absence.

Camping in a town where he believes other people are living, the man assures his son that "nothing bad is going to happen to us. . . . Because we're carrying the fire" (70). While only briefly mentioned in this passage, it is the first reference to a motif that will appear again and again in the novel, a myth the father has invented for his son to give the child a sense of meaning and purpose untouched by the evils of the world. The boy will refer to this fire on several other occasions. It evokes the Hasidic belief that worldly things and beings are "shards" in which sparks of the original divine substance lie trapped, awaiting release. Ironically, the motif also evokes the fire of the apocalypse that altered the world, as if to suggest that in the fiery ruination of the world, the few shards of divine fire (embodied in the mutual and absolute love of the father and the son) have been revealed.

After eating corncakes made from old meal found in a pantry, the boy sees what he believes to be another boy and runs after him, calling. The father, upset by his son, grabs him and prevents him from going after what he believes is an illusion or hallucination; the boy, distraught, asks what will happen to the other boy, and one senses in his cries not only the desire for friendship, which he has never really known, but also abject fear about his own tenuous condition, since he sees in this solitary boy an image of his own future without his father: "What if that little boy doesnt have anybody to take care of him? he said. What if he doesnt have a papa?" (72). The parallel between the notion of a "papa" and that of God the father is evident, and the boy's question proves to resound with practical and disturbingly theological significance as well. Although it is often the father who questions the existence of God, the boy is by no means without similar doubts in a world that presents few certainties or ready answers.

The scale and scope of the threats faced by the man and the boy increase in the next section of the book. As father and son draw closer to the southern coast, the boy's innocence suffers a profound blow. In the days that follow the encounter with the boy, the man and his son pass an orchard filled with the remains of cannibalized humans, where a row of mummified heads lines the stone wall, indicating that the practice is not haphazard or incidental but systematic and widespread. As McCarthy writes, the man had "come to see a message in each such late history, a message and a warning, and so this tableau of the slain and devoured did prove to be" (77). Father and son soon see a new group of people coming down the road, "[a]n army in tennis shoes, tramping. Carrying three-foot lengths of pipe with leather wrappings" (77). This barbaric horde, reminiscent at once of a conquering army and of the roving clans in the *Mad Max* film series, is followed by wagonloads of captured goods pulled by slaves, women enslaved and impregnated, and a line of male sex slaves tethered together by dog collars and ropes. After they pass, the father tells his son, "Yes, they were the bad guys," noting that "[t]hey're on the move. It's not a good sign" (78).

At this point in the novel, the man and the boy endure some of the harshest physical stresses they ever experience. Traveling through a snowy mountain pass, they eat nothing for days but "handfuls of the dirty snow" (86). Too weak to push it any farther, the man abandons their shopping cart; and the boy's "one last look back at the cart" (84) signals that he feels utterly displaced and dispossessed. During a sudden, heavy snowfall, with only a plastic tarp for cover and rags for shoes, they must flee a grove of trees falling around them to sleep first in a cave the father digs beneath the snow (82) and later on the road itself (86). Their suffering prompts the boy to ask his father if they are going to die, and the father is forced to admit, "Okay. I might lie" about dying, but he assures his son that "we're not dying" (86), an exchange made even more poignant later in the novel when the boy tells his father that "I always believe you . . . [because] I have to" (156). Because he is utterly dependent on his father, the boy has total faith in him, and this faith foregrounds the father's duty to be true to his child.

After waking in the road the next morning, they find footprints and wheel tracks nearby, and the man is amazed and troubled that the passers-by neither woke them nor stopped to investigate. Guessing that something dangerous is coming, he and the boy climb to high ground and wait; soon, they see two men come by, and though the father fears they have been spotted, the men pass. Having had "no food and little sleep in five days" (89), the man eventually takes the boy with him to a tall, stately house they find near the road. The description of the house evokes scenes of plantation life, and a brief reference to how "[c]hattel slaves had once trod those boards bearing food and drink on silver trays" (90) calls to mind not only the South's history of slavery but also the fiery retribution it faced in the Civil War, particularly as a result of General Sherman's infamous "March to the Sea," the Savannah campaign of 1864. Still, in a world where, as the boy remarks, "there's not any more states" (36), these references serve only to evoke the erasure of history.

The long episode at the plantation home is one of the most chilling in the novel. It features a terrifying encounter with cannibals and also shows, perversely, how one of the parental duties in this ruined world is to teach a child not just about death but about suicide. The man and his son search the house and the surrounding yard, but in the man's fatigue, he fails to notice numerous warning signs: "Piled in a window in one corner of the room was a great heap of clothing. Clothes and shoes. Belts. Coats. Blankets and old sleeping bags. He would have ample time later to think about that" (90–91). The imagery recalls the great piles of material goods taken from Jews who were shipped in railway cars to concentration camps during World War II, a reference echoed later by the father's observation that the boy "looked like something out of a deathcamp" (99). Outside the house, the man sees "a forty gallon castiron cauldron of the kind once used for rendering hogs" (92) but fails to note its greater significance and other possible use. The house, it is revealed, is the base for a group of cannibals who ambush travelers on the nearby road. After breaking through a locked trapdoor in the kitchen, the man and the boy discover that the house also contains a cellar in which prisoners are kept alive until it is time for them to be slaughtered and eaten or, in the case of a man "with his legs gone to the hip and the stumps of them blackened and burnt" (93), eaten piece by piece.

Having accidentally roused the prisoners, who beg for help and try to escape, the man and boy dash out of the cellar and close the door behind them, terrified that they will be caught and made prisoners themselves, an experience that will later trouble the boy and lead him to question whether or not he and his father are the "good guys" that they claim to be. The man and boy race out of the house and hide in the nearby woods. Certain that they will be discovered and that "This is the moment. This is the moment" (94), the father resolves to run out in the open and divert the cannibals from his son; before going, he tries to tell his son how to use the pistol to shoot himself if he is captured. But when he asks the boy if he understands, he sees nothing but the child's terrified reaction, and when the boy says, "I dont know what to do, Papa. I dont know what to do. Where will you be?" (95), the man resolves to stay by his side, forsaking a heroic self-sacrifice for the responsibility of killing his son himself, should it come to that. The tense hours as darkness falls prompt some of the father's direst questions about his duty to his son, as well as an understanding of the intense love he feels for him, all in a series of short sentences and fragments whose staccato rhythm imitates that of the man's rapidly beating heart: "What if it doesnt fire? Could you crush that beloved skull with a rock? Is there such a being within you of which you know nothing? Can there be? Hold him in your arms. Just so. The soul is quick. Pull him toward you. Kiss him. Quickly" (96).

The man and the boy stay hidden in the woods until late at night, after listening to "hideous shrieks coming from the house" (97), which the father tries to drown out by covering the boy's ears. They wander exhausted in the dark, the man carrying the boy, and after they pass out, the man leaves the boy at dawn to see if they are safe and if he can find any food, knowing that the boy will not wake and leave, since the father had "trained him to lie in the woods like a fawn" (99). The man finds an old orchard, a barn, and a house, and in his searches he discovers a packet of grape-flavored drink powder, some tools, a load of dried apples, and a reservoir of pure cold water. These small discoveries, meager by most standards, represent a sort of salvation for the man. The apple is a traditional Western symbol of knowledge and of sin; ironically, in *The Road*, where the fallen state of the world is evident and sin (in the form of violence) ever present, the dried apple serves an inverse function. It is a reminder of Eden, of the paradise of the past world, which cannot be reclaimed but elements of which can still be experienced and shared. The supplies the father finds and brings back to his son are a promise of life, however temporary and fragile, in the face of the darkness they have escaped; thus, the boy offers what is always his highest praise: "You did good Papa" (105).

In the days that follow their escape from the cannibals' house, the man and boy talk about their encounter. Though the man tries to conceal what was happening there and why they did not help the prisoners, the boy's questions force him to acknowledge that the prisoners in the cellar were meant to be eaten. Tearful, the boy says, "We wouldnt ever eat anybody, would we?" (108), and the man replies that they never would, acknowledging the boy's claims that "we're the good guys" and "we're carrying the fire" (109). This agreement to uphold the taboo against cannibalism proves a fundamental assertion of identity, morality, and goodness. That it must be overtly stated speaks to the depravity into which the world has descended in *The Road*; the fact that it is uttered speaks to the goodness of the man and his son. Yet this goodness is always under threat, and at night, the father, looking at his sleeping son, "would begin to sob uncontrollably but it wasnt about death. He wasnt sure what it was about but he thought it was about beauty or about goodnesss. Things that he'd no longer any way to think about at all" (109). No longer sure if goodness might survive in the world, the man sees "for a brief moment the absolute truth of the world. The cold relentless circling of the intestate earth. Darkness implacable. The blind dogs of the sun in their running. The crushing black vacuum of the universe. And somewhere two hunted animals trembling like ground-foxes in their cover. Borrowed time and borrowed world and borrowed eyes with which to sorrow it" (110).

The next major section of the novel provides a respite from the incessant grimness the father and son have endured up to this point. Traveling farther on, they scavenge from "the charred ruins of houses they would not have entered before" (110) but find little to take and no people anywhere. Finally, scouting one isolated house, in which they see themselves in a mirror and the man almost raises his gun to fire (111), the man and boy accidentally discover what turns out to be an underground fallout shelter, unused and well-stocked with supplies. Coming back to the house from a shed where he gathers packets of seeds, wondering "For what?" (112), the father notes a strange spot in the backyard of the house, finds a shovel, and digs until he hits a door. Though the boy is frightened and begs him not to, the father fashions a makeshift lamp and makes ready to descend, telling his son, though not before kissing him on the forehead, that "This is what the good guys do. They keep trying. They dont give up" (116). The father's kiss is a gesture of tenderness and compassion that contrasts potently with what he said earlier before descending into the cannibals' cellar, when he upbraided the boy for his fears, saying sharply, "Just stop it. We're starving. Do you understand?" (92–93). Inside the bunker, the man finds a remarkable store of canned goods, bottled water, clothing, bedding, utensils, and tools: "The richness of a vanished world," McCarthy writes (117). Overwhelmed, the man calls the boy downstairs, and they hide out in the shelter for several days.

The boy asks whether or not it is right to take the goods, but the father assures him that the people who made the shelter were "the good guys. . . . Like us" (118), and though the boy is wary that it is all just a dream, the father assures him that it is real. Taking stock of all the goods, including a handful of gold krugerands, which are now useless in a world where the need to exchange currency or gold no longer exists, and boxes of ammunition but no accompanying gun of the right caliber (120–21), the pair falls asleep, neither of them waking until the following night. The father realizes that "[h]e'd been ready to die and now he wasnt going to and he had to think about that" (121), seeing that his current situation in the shelter is more precarious than when he and the boy were living homeless, because now they are anchored to one place, suggesting that in the world of *The Road*, homelessness is the norm and the notion of a home is potentially fraught with danger.

Over breakfast, the boy asks if they should thank the people who built the bunker, and in his brief and simple grace, he reveals his innate goodness (123). Afterward, they both wash in a warm bath, leading the boy to sigh, "Warm at last" (123), which amuses the father and proves to be one of the few comic moments in the novel. Afterward, McCarthy offers a scene of peace and domestic tranquility, in which father and son, in clean clothes, play checkers and drink Coca Colas, an image reminiscent of the closing of William Shakespeare's play *The Tempest*, where the image of Ferdinand and Miranda playing chess and talking of love and faith indicates their removal from the conflict-ridden world around them. The peace of "this tiny paradise" (126), however, cannot last long in *The Road*, and the father tells his son that they cannot stay for long, fearing that someone will sneak up on them. The next day, while searching for functioning grocery carts in the nearby town, the man and the boy have a conversation in which the father says, "I dont think we're likely to meet any good guys on the road" (127), saying that "If trouble comes when you least expect it then maybe the thing to do is to always expect it" (128), a deeply pessimistic view in which their literal journey along the ever-dangerous road emerges as an emblem for existence itself. During their last days in the shelter, the man shaves his beard and cuts his and the boy's hair, fashions a portable stove burner, and readies their supplies.

The religious references evoked during the bunker episode are some of the most specifically Christian in the book. Besides serving as a sort of "Paradise regained" by the father's tenderness to the boy when they first enter the underground bunker, it also alludes to the crucifixion of Jesus, with the man and the boy being entombed or in a deathlike repose during their time there. McCarthy is attentive to the passage of time during this episode of the novel; although the total time that the man and the boy spend in the shelter is four nights and four days, the first three days offer an ironic inversion of the Easter story. Their first day in the shelter, when they are overwhelmed at their good fortune and sleep for almost 24 hours after their meal, emerges as a mirror image of the crucifixion itself, so that while each story leads to the burial of the central characters, the story of the shelter in *The Road* begins with celebration, unlike the story of Christ's death, which begins tragically with his killing. The second day, when Christ would have been in the changeless realm of the dead, the man and the boy not only feast and take pleasure in their goods, but they also improve and alter their appearances, undergoing a symbolic ritual purification (bathing, cutting hair, and shaving). On the third day, they make ready to leave, but it is not a happy or hopeful preparation, and during the night, which would conclude the full 72 hours of Christ's time among the dead, the father wakes during a rainstorm, his observations offering a darkly ironic comment on the possibility of resurrection and redemption in this world: "He could not construct for the child's pleasure the world he'd lost without constructing the loss as well and he thought perhaps the child had known this better than he. . . . Even now some part of him wished they'd never found this refuge. Some part of him always wished it to be over" (129–30).

Under way again, the father reckons they are 200 miles from the coast "as the crow flies" (131), an observation that prompts the boy to say, "There's not any crows. Are there?" (133), reminding both the father and the reader that, in *The Road*, language and words have become far removed from what they once signified or referred to, creating confusion and darkness, just like the landscape through which the man and the boy wander. The boy then tells his father that he has thrown away the carved flute he gave him, a sign that there is to be no more music in this world and that the Paradise the fallout shelter seemed to invoke is now forever lost.

Soon the man and the boy happen upon another traveler, a seemingly blind old man who fears they are robbers and says he owns nothing. The boy, eager for company and naturally inclined to charity, gives the man a can of peaches in a gesture of almost incomprehensible kindness, "like someone trying to feed a vulture broken in the road" (138). The father warns his son that they cannot "keep him" but consents to inviting the man to dinner. Walking to a campsite, the boy takes the old man's hand, though his father warns him not to, and as they walk, the old man tells them that he is 90 and that his name is Ely, an allusion to the Hebrew prophet Elijah, to whom both John the Baptist and Jesus Christ are often compared, particularly in Christ's manifestation at the Apocalypse or Judgment Day.

What follows after the dinner is the father's first long dialogue with any living character in the novel other than his son. Sitting by the campfire like a "threadbare buddha" (142), Ely says he had long predicted the destruction of the world, then speaks of how "There is no God and we are his prophets" (143), one of the clearest articulations of the novel's simultaneous disbelief in a divine presence and its fundamental reliance on—or, as could be argued, faith in—religious roles and sacraments in order to create meaning in such a nihilistic universe. Doubtful of Ely's claim that he survives through the charity of others, the father suspects Ely of being "a shill for a pack of roadagents" but relents when the old man speaks of his amazement at seeing the boy, never having "thought to see a child again," at which point the father asks, "What if I said he's a god?" (145). Ely offers that he no longer believes in gods and that if the boy is indeed the last god, then "to be on the road with the last god would be a terrible thing" (145), since, as the reader now understands, the road of existence is perilous and to witness the end of the last god would be devastating. Finally, in an echo of the poet John Donne's claim in his Holy Sonnet 6 ("Death, be not proud") that, after our deaths, "Death thou shalt die" (14), Ely says, "When we're all gone at last then there'll be nobody here but death and his days will be numbered too" (146).

The next day, Ely departs with a small gift of canned food from the boy but refuses to offer his thanks, since "I wouldnt have given him mine," nor to wish them luck, since "I dont know what that would mean. What luck would look like. Who would know such a thing?" (146). On the surface the parting seems cruel, but like the mother's final words before her suicide, it may be meant not to rouse any false hopes about a better future. The father offers that his son's motive might be that "he believes in God," and when Ely says that "[h]e'll get over it," the father promises, "No he wont" (146). Ironically, when the boy later tells his father that he is bothered by how they treated Ely, his father replies that "[t]here's not a lot of good news on the road. In times like these" (147). The father mocks Ely's intonations and offers a pun on the gospel as "good news," an indication of his continued ambivalence about the existence of God and the possibility of an inherent meaning to the universe.

Beginning the following night and continuing for the rest of the novel, the father's health, which was poor from the start, worsens, his "cold dark coughing" (148) the result of years of breathing the ashen air. Acknowledging that he is near death, he asks, "how I am going to do that" (148), a question not only about the experience of death but also an assertion of how impossible he finds it to relinquish his hold on life and thus his duty as protector of his son. Soon their conditions worsen as the boy accidentally lets the portable stove run out of fuel, and they must plod on "thin and filthy as street addicts" (149). Nevertheless, the father continues to tell his boy, "Dont lose heart. . . . We'll be all right" (149). Along the way, they find a train abandoned in the woods, and when they approach it, the father makes train noises but is not sure if the boy, who has never seen a working train, knows what they mean. Still, McCarthy notes, "If they saw different worlds what they knew was the same. That the train would sit there slowly decomposing for all eternity and no train would ever run again" (152).

As they near the coast, their supplies dwindling, the boy begins asking about the sea, wondering if it is blue and checking their location on a tattered road map. Watching his son, the man remembers his own boyhood interest in maps, how they showed "Everything in its place. Justified in the world" (154–55). During their continued travels, the father acknowledges his son's assertion that "[t]here are other good guys. You said so" (155), but his claim is immediately challenged when they encounter three men armed with lengths of pipe that the father backs down with his pistol (156). In the wake of the encounter, the father's condition worsens, and the boy fears his father is dying. During this period, both suffer painful memories and dreams, the man remembering how he once saw a den of snakes burned to death by "rough men" (159), the boy dreaming of his father's death and then of something too horrible to voice. His father tells him, "When your dreams are of some world that never was or of some world that never will be and you are happy again then you will have given up. Do you understand? And you cant give up. I wont let you" (160). This insistence that suffering and unhappiness are the only reality begins to irritate the boy, and the father recognizes "some new distance between them" (160). The boy is growing older and more independent, and his conversations with his father begin to exhibit more friction and less of the harmonious love expressed earlier in the novel; nevertheless, throughout his illness, the father knows that "[h]e was what the boy thought about" (162).

Yet the boy remains innocent, just as the world remains vile, as evidenced by a brief scene that is nevertheless one of the most shocking in the book. Worried that they are being followed, the father proposes that they head to higher ground. From there, while the boy sleeps, the father sees three men and a pregnant women pass below them on the road; two days later, they see smoke coming from the woods, and the man, fearful of being caught after passing by, takes his son into the woods to find the source. The smell proves to be a cooking fire, and as they draw close, the boy sees, before his father can shield him, "a charred human infant headless and gutless and blackening on a spit" (167). The boy cries, "Oh Papa," and the man holds him, whispering, "I'm sorry," not knowing "if he'd ever speak again" (167). Later, the boy seems increasingly withdrawn, as he seems to have stopped playing with random objects he might find on the road and refuses a ride in the shopping cart. However, when he starts out to find a nearby creek, running for the first time in a long time, the man "stop[s] and st[ands] watching, biting his lip" (169), brokenhearted by the evils his son has endured and by the boyish innocence that remains.

Soon they find another plantation-style house far off the road. Given their mixed experiences with the cannibals' household and the fallout shelter, they approach it with trepidation. As they walk, the father finds two arrowheads and a coin with Spanish lettering, which he holds out to the boy, but such artifacts, he realizes, are not only meaningless, but they are not interesting to someone who has never known the world they came from. The boy reluctantly enters the house, and as they search it, they discover several dozen jars of canned goods, which they worry may be spoiled but which they nonetheless decide to try to cook and eat, given their circumstances. Later, as they did at the bunker, the man and boy find useful goods in the house (including blankets, a saw, and a wagon) and take baths. The new shelter is like the old one, though not as well-stocked and less accommodating. Nevertheless, the boy says, "We did good, didnt we Papa?" (180), showing that even as he grows older and understands more of the evil of the world, he can still be grateful.

Throughout this section of the novel, McCarthy presents images suggesting reversion and the possibility of lapsing back into a primitive past even worse than the present. On their travels to the coast, the two stop at an old filling station to draw up cupfuls of gas from old wells "like apes fishing with sticks in an anthill" (181). As the father's health continues to decline, so that he coughs at night "like a man waking in a grave" (180), he remembers how, long ago, he saw disinterred cholera victims with the antique copper pennies falling from their eyes, a reference to the custom of burying the dead with money to pay the ferryman Charon during their crossing into the Underworld. The image suggests that no such funds remain and that the dead do not disappear but go on haunting the world in a half-alive state, reflective of the father's own. Still, the father seems to understand and resist this reversion. One night, after putting the boy to bed in the house and falling asleep himself at the dining table while keeping watch, he wakes, banks the fire, and muses on the possibility that the divine might exist and that it might be concerned with this basic show of human love: "They are watching for a thing even death cannot undo and if they do not see it they will turn away from us and they will not come back" (177).

Finally, they reach the sea. Though the man had held out hope that it might be in a better state of preservation than the interior of the country through which they have passed, it is just as compromised and altered:

> Out there was the gray beach with the slow combers rolling dull and leaden and the distant sound of it. Like the desolation of some alien sea breaking on the shores of a world unheard of. Out on the tidal flats lay a tanker half careened. Beyond that the ocean vast and cold and shifting heavily like a slowly heaving vat of slag and then the gray squall line of ash. (181)

After their initial disappointment, the boy and his father sit on the beach, speculating how on the other side of the ocean there might be another father and son also carrying the fire, also wondering if anything existed on the far shore. Though the father says that they have to be vigilant, he tells the son that he should go swimming in the ocean, and the boy runs "naked and leaping and screaming into the slow roll of the surf" (184), a moment of joy in the face of the world's blankness. After drying and warming him, the father sees that the boy is crying; McCarthy does not make it clear if the tears are prompted because the world has failed him utterly or if, in its own strange way, it has provided him some consolation in spite of itself. In the following days, the man and boy find the coast "one vast salt sepulchre, senseless" (187), in contrast to the father's memory of sleeping with his wife on the beach, when he decided that "if he were God he would have made the world just so and no different" (185).

The day after their arrival, the man and boy find a long sailboat stranded just offshore, and after scouting the area for other people, the man decides to swim out to the ship and search it for supplies. In a gesture reminiscent of his earlier descent into the bunker, the man kisses the worried boy before he swims naked out to the ship, which is named *Pájaro de Esperanza* ("Bird of Hope") and is out of Tenerife in the Canary Islands, suggesting not only that the disaster impacted Europe as well but that any hope for the future has itself been shipwrecked. Inside the ship, the man finds many ruined goods but also some good clothing to change into. When he goes on deck to signal to the boy his safe arrival, he realizes that "in his new clothes he made an uncertain figure" (190), but his calls to the boy go unheard over the wind and distance; the image of this incommunicable distance seems to imply the growing separation between the two and also foreshadows the final rift created by death.

From the hold of the ship, the father gathers various useful items, including clothing, tools, bottles of gas, food, and a working stove burner, but most surprising is the antique brass sextant he discovers, which leaves him "[s]truck by the beauty of it. . . . It was the first thing he'd seen in a long time that stirred him" (192). The sextant is a reminder of the possibility of beauty in the world but also, because the man puts it back where he found it without ever showing it to his son, of the extinction of beauty and the near impossibility of navigating or charting a definable course in this greatly altered environment. After he swims back to shore with the goods, the father and boy set out for their campsite; along the way, the boy realizes he has forgotten the pistol, which they locate after a hasty search. On their way back, they are overtaken by the dark. A storm begins, and the father's command, "Don't let go. . . . No matter what" (197), makes the scene a summary of their struggle to survive the postapocalyptic world and of their undying connection to and protection of each other. Amid the lightning and rainfall, they are guided back to their site by the sound of rain hitting the tarp.

When they wake the next morning, the father sees an ancient corpse in the shallows and wishes he could hide it from the boy but grimly realizes there is no longer any point in protecting him. They spend the morning offloading the ship, and in the days that follow, they continue simply to endure in their meager, comfortless fashion. The father grows increasingly sick, now coughing blood, and his bitterness at the futility of their struggle grows: "Every day is a lie, he said. But you are dying. That is not a lie" (200). Making one last trip out to the sailboat, the man finds a two-person raft, oars, a first-aid kit, flares, and a flare pistol, which he will use to make a new weapon. Discussing the matter later, the boy wonders about the fate of the ship passengers and concludes that they must have died; he no longer holds out hope for happy endings as he once did, and though the man at first tries to say they could be alive, he finally acknowledges that the boy is right. This prompts the boy to wonder if there might be another planet where they might go to live, and when the father says that they could not live anywhere else, the boy responds, echoing his mother's despair, "I dont know what we're doing" (206), stunning the father to silence before he repeats the illusory hope that others might still be alive. Later, the boy asks about writing a letter to the good guys in the sand, but when the father asks about the bad guys who might read it, the boy drops the subject, a scene that illustrates the uselessness, even the danger, of writing and communication in the world they inhabit.

That night, the father shoots the flare gun for the boy, who realizes how hard it would be for anyone—a good guy or God—to find them; the next morning, the boy falls ill with fever and nausea, and the father enters a period of heightened tension. While the earlier encounters with the cannibals had put both their lives at risk and forced the father to confront the possibility of having to kill his own son to protect him, the boy's illness is a slower but no less lethal threat, leaving the father to his own bleak meditations as he concludes, "I will do what I promised. . . . No matter what. I will not send you into the darkness alone" (209). The father's spiritual agonies, his sense that this is the "[l]ast day of the earth" (210), are relieved when the boy wakes, feeling whole but "kind of weird" (212) and unwilling to speak of his "weird dreams" (212), his recovery a form of resurrection. The next few days are taken up with preparations to depart and with the father staring with an unspoken intensity at this boy who has been safely delivered.

Returning to their base camp one evening, they discover that their cart and all their possessions have been stolen. Finding that the thief's tracks end at the road, they search carefully for any trace of sand that might have fallen from the cart and, finding it, set off to recover their goods. After an hour, they catch a man with "the fingers of his right hand . . . cut away," a sign that he is "an outcast from one of the communes" (215) but also, allusively, that he is a figure for Cain, who killed his brother Abel and was marked by God so that he might wander forever but be left untouched by others. Though he wields a butcher knife, he drops it when the father cocks and aims the pistol; crying, the boy pleads with his father not to kill the man, but the father orders the thief to strip off all his clothes, though the thief begs, "Come on, man. I'll die" (217). They leave him "[a] nude and slatlike creature standing there in the road shivering and hugging himself" (217).

In the wake of this encounter, the conversations between the man and his son intensify for the duration of the novel, often addressing major moral and spiritual questions. Their conversation after abandoning the thief, for instance, signals a major shift in terms of the moral authority in their relationship. Distraught by the thief's plight, the boy says that he wants his father to "just help him," a command for charity that the father cannot honor, saying that "I'm scared. . . . You're not the one who has to worry about everything" (218). The boy ends their exchange by saying that "I am the one" (218), a claim signaling that, just as the father has responsibility for their physical survival, so the son has responsibility for the goodness of their souls. Some scholars have claimed that the language implies the boy is accepting the Christ role that his father had previously granted him; at the very least, the child understands that, never having known the world as it was, he must inherit the ruined world as it is and thus must be "the one" who creates and establishes goodness in the new world. In response, the father agrees to return and aid the man, but failing to find him, they can only leave his clothes and shoes in a pile in the road, leaving the boy to say that "we did kill him" (219). This admission, coming so soon after the boy's assumption of a Christ role, culminates in McCarthy's chilling claim that "The salitter [was] drying from the earth" (220), a word borrowed from the seventeenth-century German mystic Jakob Boehme that means "the essence of God." McCarthy uses the term to suggest the withdrawal of the divine from existence.

The father's increasingly ominous sense that his own death "is coming to steal my eyes. To seal my mouth with dirt" (220) comes true in the final section of the novel. As the man and boy walk through a port town, they are attacked by a bowman, and as the man pulls his son down for cover, an arrow pierces his leg. Taking aim, he fires the flare gun at the bowman in a nearby window, and when he limps into the house, he finds that the bow has apparently been taken by others and that a woman has chosen to stay beside the man's dead body (an act of self-sacrifice, perhaps, because she is defenseless). Soon thereafter, the man finds a building where he can tend to his wounds; afterward, when the father offers to tell his son a story, the two speak of the nature of storytelling, with the boy claiming that the father's stories are all happy, while his own are "more like real life" (226). This acknowledgment that the father's representation of the world is a hopeful fiction is part of a growing stoicism on the boy's part, an acceptance that life is "pretty bad" (226). Yet in spite of this maturation (and, one might say, growing despair), the father still lies to his son to suggest the notion of a better future. The father says that his wound, despite its dreadful appearance, will heal, and when asked if he killed the man with the bow, he says he did not. Perhaps having failed his son in so many ways, it seems, he cannot bear to do so again, or perhaps he means to suggest that the thief's death was not the result of an individual action but of fate itself.

The two press on, now simply wandering with no destination, a powerful symbol of the existential crisis engendered by the world's devastation; when asked by his son, "What is the bravest thing you ever did," the father replies, "Getting up this morning" (229). He is growing sicker and weaker, but in consequence, because no meaningful world exists beyond their bond, the boy cleaves to him entirely, a pure and intense love that is perhaps the only positive element to emerge from all the destruction McCarthy has depicted. Thus, when the father looks at the boy, he sees him "glowing in that waste like a tabernacle" (230), the "fire" that he once carried now transfigured into the pure light of the divine.

Soon they reach "a broad tidal river where the bridge lay collapsed in the slow moving water" (232), perhaps the Mississippi River, but in a symbolic sense, Styx, the river of the dead, for when they stop at an inland crossroads a few days later, the father knows "that he could go no further and that this was the place where he would die" (233). When he looks at his son, the father now sees the boy haloed in light, and he is moved to acknowledge the continued presence of the divine in the world: "Look around you. . . . There is no prophet in the earth's long chronicle who's not honored here today. Whatever form you spoke of you were right" (233). Yet this persistence of the divine has been achieved by their own mutual, human love; the "form you spoke of" is a tacit reference to God's utterance of the divine Word (or Logos) during creation, but since the Word also stands for Jesus, the son of God, then the father is suggesting not that he is divine but that what he and his son have achieved—sustaining their love for each other in a world void of meaning—is as profound as creation itself.

The passages that follow are mostly dialogue between the father and son, and they are at once painfully sorrowful and uncompromisingly uplifting, with the father speaking with his son about death, the hereafter, the path the boy must follow and the good luck he is sure to find, and, finally, about the father's absolute love for his son. "You have my whole heart. You always did. You're the best guy" (235), he tell his son. It is perhaps the most beautiful passage in the entire novel, rendered in the same spare, poetic language McCarthy has used throughout, a scene of tenderness, compassion, and love that could not be achieved without the backdrop of darkness and desolation that *The Road* has wrought in hellish detail. The father teaches his son to pray, saying that "If I'm not here you can still talk to me. You can talk to me and I'll talk to you. You'll see" (235), and finally, in his last words, offers a blessing that recalls the lost boy from earlier in the novel, whom the man's son had wanted to find and protect precisely because he could recognize the other boy's plight as his own: "Goodness will find the little boy. It always has. It always will" (236). The man dies in the night, and the boy kneels beside him, saying "his name over and over again" (236), a name that the reader never hears but that assures us that, through his love, this man fashioned an identity, a self, a soul for himself, and that in the desolation of the world's ending, his life meant something.

One might marvel how, at this moment of greatest pathos, the novel also achieves its greatest uplift, its haunting sense that goodness will indeed find the lost boy. As reviewer Todd Shy writes, "Only at the last minute does the bleakness sit up and offer a deathbed declaration, and the success of the novel depends on whether this conclusion is convincing" (38). For Shy, the conclusion does not convince: "These last eight pages of *the Road* are . . . startling, and the optimism—grittier than the final chapter of Job, but similarly incongruous—is emotionally understandable, yet artistically unearned" (41). Yet perhaps this scene reveals the love and goodness with which the universe began: "Perhaps in the world's destruction it would be possible at last to see how it was made" (230–31). McCarthy's characteristic syntactical device of offering a memory or a word only to show how the thing to which it refers is absent and lost suggests that what is witnessed in the boy's final exchanges with his father is, in fact, the end of love. Still, the novel depicts a possible future, and in doing so, by presenting absence, it confirms the very presence of that which was believed lost; by showing the reader what might be the last instance of a good, holy love left in the ruined world of *The Road*, McCarthy demands that the reader acknowledge and embrace all such instances of love in the world of the present, the known world, which has not yet been destroyed.

In a sense, the brief events that follow the father's death enact this transformation of the loss of love into an affirmation of its presence, while also fulfilling the father's promise that the boy would be lucky and that goodness would find him. The boy stays to grieve by his father's side three days, an allusion to the three days of Christ's death and resurrection, which had also been hinted at during their time in the bunker but which had culminated not in resurrection but in the father's wish that they had never found that "tiny paradise" (126), since they would only have to give it up. Now, however, the boy meets a man coming down the road, "a veteran of old skirmishes" (237) who has been following him and now, learning of the father's death, offers to take him into his family (along with his wife, son, and daughter), if only the boy will trust him. "How do I know if you're one of the good guys?" the boy asks. "You dont. You'll have to take a shot" (238), answers the man, calling on the boy to have faith—in family and community, in goodness—and, in a sense, reasserting and restoring the validity of such bonds and virtues in the world. The boy accepts but, before leaving, goes to visit his father's body once more, which the veteran wraps in a blanket. It is a gesture of respect for the body of the dead that has been previously unknown in the novel's bestial world of cannibals. Crying, the boy promises, "I'll talk to you every day. . . . And I wont forget. No matter what" (240–41), a promise of love that validates memory itself, which the father had once thought too harmful in this world, since memory could make one continually suffer the pain of loss. Still, the son's promise demonstrates that, without memory, goodness and love could not be preserved.

The concluding two paragraphs embody the duality of presence and absence that McCarthy has embodied throughout the novel. In the penultimate paragraph, McCarthy writes that the veteran's wife "would talk to him sometimes about God" but that he found it easier to talk to his father, and she affirms the value of his manner of prayer, saying, "that the breath of God was his breath yet though it pass from man to man through all of time" (241), a claim that unites the divine and eternal (the breath of God) with the physical and historical (man, all of time), a union often identified with the incarnation of God into the human form of Jesus. The final paragraph, however, offers a sense of finality to balance the eternal continuation suggested by the woman's words. In this paragraph, the narrator describes brook trout in the mountains, an echo of the father's earlier memories of trout and also an allusion to the trout in Ernest Hemingway's "Big Two-Hearted River," which become symbols of the individual's drive to hold steady amid the exigencies of time. "On their backs were vermiculate patterns that were maps of the world in its becoming," McCarthy writes, "Maps and mazes. Of a thing that could not be put back. Could not be made right again" (241). While the notion that the world cannot be put back or made right offers a bleak final comment on the future awaiting the boy and the remaining survivors in *The Road*, it is also a stoic affirmation that the world must be faced and lived in as it is. From a differing perspective, however, the final paragraph seems to speak of the world's perfect vulnerability, suggesting not that it has already been ruined but that it could be, and that if it were, it could not recover. The novel's concluding lines serve as McCarthy's parting comment on nature, on human relationships, and on faith itself, a confirmation of their value and a plea for their protection.

Critical Views

TODD SHY ON *THE ROAD,* THE BOOK OF JOB, AND QUESTIONS ABOUT EVIL

The Book of Job feels unnecessarily long, but we tolerate the repetition because the final payoff is powerful. Along the way, the arguments against Job form concentric cages of folly, cant, common sense and basic theology, and Job must either accept being their prisoner or stage some kind of personal break. *The Road* is not a modern retelling of the biblical poem, but in its repetitious gloom, its relentless punishment of the main characters and, most important, the lateness of its rupture it mirrors Job's trajectory. In Job, it is chapter 38 of 42 before God interrupts the human debate and declaims from the whirlwind; the departure in *The Road*—a final human affirmation—begins somewhere around page 233 of 241. Up to that point, Cormac McCarthy's tale is patient to the point of being hypnotic, and the story enacts its own slow expiration. Only at the last minute does the bleakness sit up to offer a deathbed declaration, and the success of the novel depends on whether this conclusion is convincing.

The Road tracks the journey of an unnamed father and son as they wander across a postapocalyptic wasteland. Though we never learn exactly what calamity has transpired, the landscape is utterly ruined and covered in ash. Wildlife is absent, and the surviving human population is so sparse and desolate that every remote stranger is both competitor and threat. Pushing a shopping cart of salvaged possessions with a direction in mind (south) but no real destination (there is no safe place to go), father and son make the dangerous passage speaking essentially only to each other. On the way they discover a bomb shelter with a cache of canned food, a man burned by a lightning strike, prisoners huddled against the approach of their cannibal captors, an ash-shrouded locomotive, a nearly blind old man who tries to steal their supplies, numerous corpses (including, most gruesomely, a charred infant on a campfire spit), and a small boy they cannot help, whose memory haunts the son to the end of the novel. The horror, in other words, is unrelieved, and we feel that McCarthy, our great chronicler of violence, is filling out his oeuvre with a projection of ultimate destruction.

In the wake of apocalypse, reconstituting human life is a grim, uncertain business. McCarthy's fragmented style throughout suggests that human speech and human narrative must also—like other primitive skills—be reconstituted. And so the code of simple survival for his characters has as its analogue the pared-down, halting, mythical rhythms of the prose. In those places where the language is both beautiful and terrifying, the parallel is just right: "Perhaps in the world's destruction it would be possible at last to see how it was made. Oceans, mountains. The ponderous counterspectacle of things ceasing to be. The sweeping waste, hydroptic and coldly secular. The silence. . . .

. . . The most critical component in *The Road* is the relationship between the father and his son. At one level they embody a very simple instinct: the unconquerable love between parent and child. And when the boy proves to be more sensitive than his father toward strangers in need, we see another primitive instinct—that of childlike simplicity, in all its generosity and naïveté. But there is a shadow side to their relationship. The boy's mother committed suicide before they set out, and the father has clearly pondered whether to kill both his son and himself rather than succumb to postapocalypse predation. In this respect, their journey is a darker version of Abraham and Isaac's. The father, like Abraham, packs a weapon, but here both father and son may be sacrificed before an inscrutable, destructive god.

Yet when the dying father—whose pistol always has two bullets at the ready—must send his son out on his own, he refuses Abraham's terrible gesture: "I cant [sic]. I cant hold my son dead in my arms. I thought I could but I cant." With this dying scene—the last eight pages of the book—McCarthy evokes an improbable vision of redemption and goodness. Telling his son that he must "carry the fire" and find "the good guys," he assures him that he will be spared. And when the son mentions again the lost boy they could not help, the father offers lofty reassurance: "Goodness will find the little boy. It always has. It will again."

This would all be understandable deathbed sentiment were it not for the book's swift conclusion. After the father dies, a family of the good guys immediately rescues the son, and as he joins them back on the road, the mother teaches the boy that "the breath of God was his breath yet though it pass from man to man through all time." McCarthy ends the narrative with a description of a natural world that is older than human dilemmas and that "hummed of mystery."

Nothing has prepared us for this abrupt suggestion of hope. The boy's goodness throughout is innocent rather than prophetic. Nothing has encouraged a belief that the good guys might reconstitute the earth. These last eight pages of *The Road* are therefore startling, and the optimism—grittier than the final chapter of Job, but similarly incongruous—is emotionally understandable, yet artistically unearned. The frisson of Abraham raising the knife and the friction between Jehovah and Job dissolve here in the elegant cadences of McCarthy's vision. It seems stingy to criticize the flash of hope; who doesn't want the world, in the end, to hum with mystery? But we need the mystery to pull us through by confronting the horror. Sidestepped, it can't assure us of its triumph.

THOMAS A. CARLSON ON McCARTHY'S EXISTENTIAL THEMES

The Road engages us in a meditation—both literary and religious—on the essential interplay of world and heart. It does so, I aim to show here, as if in a phenomenological experience akin to those I've signaled with boredom and anxiety; or as if in a crisis of heart like that which was crucial in Augustine's life and thought. That is, it does so by staging the suspension of world through a narrative of nearly complete catastrophe and pervasive peril. Radically deprived of the things and persons in relation with which and with whom one normally exists, those who travel *The Road* find themselves and their existence thrown into absolute question, like Augustine upon the death of his friend, and confronting, like Dasein in its fundamental anxiety, the dark nothingness of their world. In light of that darkness, without access to the normal supports for a flight and falling in which one might comfortably dwell, the travelers of *The Road* are thrown back upon themselves and confronted, if only through an absence or failure, with the barest, essential conditions of their worldly life and its possibility—conditions now illuminated by their very darkening.[28]

The Road tells the tale of an unnamed but sickly and struggling father and son who walk slowly south and toward an unnamed coast across an unnamed but devastated, dying, and deadly landscape where other people are few and those who do appear represent first and foremost the threat of torment and death, as by blood cult and cannibalism. A sense of the radical suspension that structures the entire work—and an evocation of the paradoxes entailed in telling the story of such suspension—appear in their key elements within a passage toward the end of the work, after father and son have reached that coast which stood throughout their journey as the only spoken destination other than death itself, and which now—having been reached—reveals to them an ocean vast, cold and gray, "like the desolation of some alien sea breaking on the shores of a world unheard of" (*R* 181):

> He [the father] got up and walked out to the road. The black shape of it running from dark to dark. Then a distant low rumble. Not thunder. You could feel it in your feet. A sound without cognate and so without description. Something imponderable shifting out there in the dark. The earth itself contracting with the cold. It did not come again. What time of year? What age the child? He walked out into the road and stood. The silence. The salitter drying from the earth. The mudstained shapes of flooded cities burned to the waterline. At a crossroads a ground

set with dolmen stones where the spoken bones of oracles lay moldering. No sound but the wind. What will you say? A living man spoke these lines? He sharpened a quill with his small pen knife to scribe these things in sloe or lampblack? At some reckonable and entabled moment? He is coming to steal my eyes. To seal my mouth with dirt. (*R* 220)

This one passage brings to expression quite effectively the key elements of the work that will inform my reading: a pervasive darkness and its association with the un-nameable, imponderable, and singular (from dark to dark . . . sound without cognate); the flattening or un-differentiation of a time that has in some way ceased, or that persists unmarked and unrecorded (what time of year, what age the child); the silence of a world in the midst of its death, both natural and social (the earth itself, the flooded cities); the interplay of memory and expectation or anticipation (dolmen stones and spoken bones)—and in light of all this darkness, where such memory and expectation may be deprived of their very conditions by an absolute death, the question of language and story.

What become of time and language, of life and story, in the presence of such darkness, in the seeming collapse of world, or in the withdrawal of that possibility we might take to make a world? What role would memory and expectation—the marking of years and ages—have played in sustaining the time and language of a world sufficiently living to bear (or to be born by) the telling of a story? And how might all of this relate to the human heart?

The work opens straightaway in a night "dark beyond darkness" (*R* 3) with the man and his sleeping child who walk together, "each the other's world entire" (*R* 5) through days "more gray each one than what had gone before. Like the onset of some cold glaucoma dimming away the world" (*R* 3). The father "thought if he lived long enough the world at last would all be lost. Like the dying world the newly blind inhabit, all of it slowly fading from memory" (*R* 16).[29] In this opening and throughout, the work stages the spectacle of a world's closing or disappearance; it narrates the radical cessation or suspension of time itself, its flattening into a monotony that threatens all anticipation and recollection—and it makes such closing and disappearance, such cessation and suspension, along with the mortality these signal, a matter of the heart: "He lay listening to the water drip in the woods. Bedrock, this. The cold and the silence. The ashes of the late world carried on the bleak and temporal winds to and fro in the void. Carried forth and scattered and carried forth again. Everything uncoupled from its shoring. Unsupported in the ashen air. Sustained by a breath, trembling and brief. If only my heart were stone" (*R* 11). His heart, however, is not stone, nor is it even his own. The heart, in whose light alone any possibility of world or life at all appear for him belongs not to him, alone, but to his being-with the fragile and threatened child who himself never knew the world—having been born only after the unnamed catastrophe, and thereby opening, or incarnating, the question of what birth and its promise could mean in the ostensible absence of any time for expectation or memory. He looks upon the boy— "ghostly pale and shivering," "so thin it stopped his heart" (*R* 33)—and he thinks, "So thin. My heart, he said. My heart. But he knew that if he were a good father still it might be as she [the mother] had said. That the boy was all that stood between him and death" (*R* 25). The promise of a birth and its life, appearing in the ostensible absence of the conditions for any promise or life, is the heart that holds death at bay. Can such a heart still sustain a world? What could it mean to have a heart, or to care for a child, without a world? Or what could it mean to have a world without such a heart? "Not all dying words are true," the father suggests, "and this blessing is no less real for being shorn of its ground" (*R* 26).

The mother, to whom this passage refers, also made, in light of the world's darkening and of death's pervasive presence, a linkage between her heart and the child. "You talk about taking a stand," she says to the man in explaining her decision for suicide instead of survival, but there is no stand to take. My heart was ripped out of me the night he was born so don't ask for sorrow now. There is none. Maybe you'll be good at this. I doubt it, but who knows. The one thing I can tell you is that you won't survive for yourself. I know because I would never have come this far. A person who had no one would be well advised to cobble together some passable ghost. Breathe it into being and coax it along with words of love. Offer it each phantom crumb and shield it from harm with your body. As for me my only hope is for eternal nothingness and I hope it with all my heart. (*R* 48–9)

The mother's hopelessness, the failure of her heart, or the turn of her heart toward that darkness and death in which sorrowing itself is swallowed up,[30] relate fundamentally if negatively to the question of world and time and their founding conditions in the openness of a possibility, which means a futurity and its past, that simply no longer appears to her. In the absolute closure of such possibility, in the total presence of death, she suggests, there is not only no life to live or love but also—what amounts to the same—nothing more to say, no story still to tell. "We used to talk about death," she says to the man in discussing her decision for suicide. "We don't anymore. Why is that? I don't know. It's because it's here. There's nothing left to talk about" (*R* 48). To have something still to talk about, the mother suggests, articulating a key theme of the work, would be to have a life and a world whose temporality could sustain—or be sustained by—a heart.

What, according to *The Road*, does it really mean to have a world in this sense? The work responds to this question—it illuminates for us the world-hood of the world——mainly, as I'm suggesting, by staging the world's suspension, which here means the near total collapse or negation of our being-alongside things ready to hand (the tools and networks through which we pursue the projects of daily life); the failure of our being-with others (who alone could make sense of such projects by sharing them); and a loss of what would have been the essential co-implication between these two as sustained temporally through the dynamic and open interplay between a forward looking memory and a recollective anticipation.

The scope and significance of the loss entailed in a world's collapse are lit up with remarkable intensity and in various ways throughout the work, both in terms of absence or decline and in terms of exceptional presence. This latter is seen, for example, late in the story when the man and child—starving and at their nearest yet to death—come haphazardly, in a random backyard, upon a hidden underground bunker that holds in store, and in what seems abundance, the fruits of a now barren earth, along with the implements born of a sociality now missing. Beholding the array of foods and tools standing there in reserve, outside the world that yielded them, the father says in answer to the child's question, "What did you find?": "I found everything. Everything. Wait till you see" (*R* 117). In other words: "the richness of a vanished world" (*R* 117). Such richness, of course, appears in the novel less often through such nourishing and sustaining presence—which is itself, in the scope of things, perhaps to be lamented insofar as it may only forestall the inevitable[31]—and more often through the vanishing or decline, through the negative image or trace: newspapers, billboards, and advertisements; money and markets and stores; telephones and their books; cars and trains and their now pointless, empty routes: everything seems like a message or a means of exchange and connection now shorn of sender and purpose, bereft of any recipient or destination but nonetheless present in its inoperative, but still visible, possibility. Goods and values, plans and projects, hopes and promises all still appear—their intentions and means, tokens and aims persist—but in light of their now withdrawn possibility, in the failure of the world, and of the interplay between memory and expectation, that sustained them.

Recalling the "living death" of worldly time in Augustine, where the genuine future is closed out by the deadly recurrence of sin, the flattened and monotonous time of *The Road* marks a suspension of living temporality that illuminates, through the suspension itself, the character of such temporality. However, if those who walk in *The Road* may be already dead, they would be such, I'd say, less because, as in Augustine, they love the world and dwell there in the heart and more because, to the contrary, they have been deprived of the things and persons whose interrelations would form a world where a living temporality—and the love tied to it—could remain operative. At several points, the work evokes this eclipse or closure of worldly memory and expectation and of the sociality they entail in temporal terms that recall, as in another perverse imitation, the eternity of Augustine's otherworldly God. "On this road," the narrative voice notes, "there are no godspoke men. They are gone and I am left and they have taken with them the world. Query: How does the never to be differ from what never was?" (R 27).[32] As this passage suggests, the "was" of a living memory would be required by any truly vital "to be," and these depend on our being-with those others who in *The Road* have "taken with them the world" (R 27). Our memory of ancestors who would have looked toward us without ever comprehending us, and our anticipation of heirs who might recall us in ways that we will never know, fail here in their essential interplay.[33] "Do you think that your fathers are watching? That they weigh you in their ledgerbook? Against what? There is no book and your fathers are dead in the ground" (R 165). To live still, in a world, *The Road* suggests, would mean still to inhabit, or incarnate, this dynamic and irreducibly open interplay between anticipation and memory. It is in a world-less world, as revealed by *The Road*, a world without possibility of such memory or anticipation, that "the days sloughed past uncounted and uncalendared. Along the interstate in the distance long lines of charred and rusting cars. . . . The incinerate corpses shrunk to the size of a child . . . Ten thousand dreams ensepulchred within their crozzled hearts. They went on. Treading the dead world under like rats on a wheel. The nights dead still and deader black. So cold. They talked hardly at all" (R 230).

The "frailty of everything" in *The Road* is seen to be, like the possibility of everything which its frailty and failure illuminate, the function of this temporality now radically suspended or flattened and of the sociality attendant to such temporality. In the first years post-catastrophe, we learn, the roads were peopled with refugees shrouded up in their clothing. . . . Towing wagons or carts. Their eyes bright in their skulls. Creedless shells of men tottering down the causeways like migrants in a feverland. The frailty of everything revealed at last. Old and troubling issues resolved into nothingness and night. The last instance of a thing takes the class with it. Turns out the light and is gone. Look around you. Ever is a long time. But the boy knew what he knew. That ever is no time at all. (*R* 24)

"Everything," the work suggests, fails absolutely, resolves into nothingness and night, insofar as it is consumed by such a timeless time of "ever," the time of no time that we might believe operative not only in death "itself" but indeed in the living death of a life without that shared openness of future and past, a living death wherein one would find "no lists of things to be done. The day providential to itself. The hour. There is no later. This is later" (*R* 46).

Of course, the father's whole struggle is to resist the admission—which he thus also must entertain—that there is no later, and here we might perhaps note one part of his difference from the mother. The father wants to insist that they—mother, father and child—are survivors, which would mean that they have some warrant to go on, or to hope; the mother, by contrast, believes they are not survivors but walking dead, without any such warrant or hope because without any future other than a certain death that is in fact not future but already fully present. This difference between the two is not unshakable, and, indeed the poignancy of the father's position has everything to do with his capacity to see the mother's view: the central anticipation of his journey's time is, after all, the anticipation of a moment when he would have to kill his son so as to spare the son some greater horror. "Can you do it?" he asks himself with an urgency that recalls 1 John's last hour, "When the time comes? When the time comes there will be no time. Now is the time. Curse God and die . . ." (*R* 96).

The fact is, however—and the very telling of the story can be read as attestation of this—that father and son do not quite live in a time of no time; and death is not quite wholly and, as the mother says, already here. The reader can see this because the disappearance of worldly things and persons, and the closing of worldly time, are held open here in their appearance. The suspension of the world—held up here as story—is not an absolute darkness but the illumination of a darkness, the appearance of a disappearance that itself (the disappearance) serves to highlight a founding possibility and condition of all appearance—and indeed the power of every birth: that, in its essential vulnerability, it well could have not been, and could yet cease to be. If at a certain point the father realizes that "he could not construct for the child's pleasure the world he'd lost without constructing the loss as well" (R 129), this realization states in reverse direction a guiding insight of the work, as stated pointedly toward its end: "Perhaps in the world's destruction it would be possible at last to see how it was made. Oceans, mountains. The ponderous counterspectacle of things ceasing to be" (R 230–31).[34] The construction or creation and the loss—both in and of this work—are co-implicated.

What is it whose ceasing would mean the ceasing of things to be? Perhaps above all, as I'm suggesting, the forms of anticipation and memory that stem from, even as they may be understood to sustain, the possibility, or the hope, of a love that would be of and for the world. At any number of points, the novel evokes this play of anticipation and memory, as well as their ties to love, by reference to message and signal, to books and stories—including this story itself, as suggested in my long opening quote from the novel.

Along the road, "hopeless messages to loved ones lost and dead" (R 152) appear alongside warnings of death from the long departed. A flare gun appears mainly as weapon, because it seems "there's nobody to signal" (R 203). We sense the despair when we learn the child knows his alphabet, but does not work on his lessons anymore (R 206). In this nearly world-less world and nearly timeless time, where there remains perhaps nobody to signal, all of language, any potential sign, any message of warning or, above all, any message of love—which really means all of the world—can be seen now, in their inoperative persistence, to have been the function of a promise, and a memory, likewise vanishing:

> So little of promise in that country. . . . He tried to think of something to say but he could not. He'd had this feeling before, beyond the numbness and the dull despair. The world shrinking down about a raw core of parsible entities. The names of things slowly following those things into oblivion. Colors, the names of birds. Things to eat. Finally the names of things one believed to be true. More fragile than he would have thought. How much was already gone? The sacred idiom shorn of its referents and so of its reality. Drawing down like something trying to preserve heat. In time to wink out forever. (*R* 74–5)

The world shrinks insofar as promise, and memory, fade, insofar as the open structures and temporality of being-with-others, thanks to whom alone beings-ready-to-hand remain significant, collapse and threaten to close altogether.

In one key passage along these lines, the man's "dreams brightened" and "the vanished world returned" and "kin long dead washed up" and he stands by a window watching the street below on a "gray day in a foreign city" and on the table behind him "books and papers" and at the table "a woman" (*R* 157). The scene, so far, recalls what elsewhere the father remembers of a night with his wife by the sea, about which he said "if he were God he would have made the world just so and no different" (*R* 185). But then: "Years later," the narrative suddenly shifts,

> he'd stood in the charred ruins of a library where blackened books lay in pools of water. Shelves tipped over. Some rage at the lies arranged in their thousands row on row. He picked up one of the books and thumbed through the heavy bloated pages. He'd not have thought the value of the smallest thing predicated on a world to come. It surprised him. That the space which these things occupied was itself an expectation. He let the book fall

and took a last look around and made his way out into the
cold gray light. (*R* 157–58)

The space of this written and once living memory, the library
as it appears here in its ruin, was essentially—and the ruin itself
illuminates this—a space of expectation. From the perspective opened here, by this story of the failure and fall of books
and their possibility, to speak of a "world to come" may well
be redundant, insofar as the open expectation of what is yet to
come, an expectation sustained only by living memory (which
means a memory that is non-automatic, not assured, and thus
subject to loss), would alone give a world in which one might
hope to live, or be able to love.

That hope, note, might imply also an essential sorrow—or a
sorrow that is itself condition of hope, insofar as the capacity to
sorrow would itself require (much as with world and its suspension) the persistence, even if through its negative appearance,
of that possibility whose loss sorrows us.[35] Here we could perhaps see another difference between the father and the mother.
If the mother, as we saw, refuses the possibility of sorrow that is
because she cannot see the possibility of hope, which is to say
that she cannot see any openness for time or world to come.
The father, by contrast, in the very recognition of pervasive
danger and of the threat of absolute loss, lives in the hope
whose possibility is implied by sorrow itself—which is to say
the hope implied by world and by its truth, which is revealed
through the negative possibility of its suspension, where it
appears not as self-evident but as contingent, like a gift:

They scrabbled through the charred ruins of houses they
would not have entered before. A corpse floating in the
black water of a basement among the trash and rusting
ductwork. He stood in a living room partly burned and
open to the sky. The waterbuckled boards sloping away
into the yard. Soggy volumes in a bookcase. He took one
down and opened it and then put it back. Everything
damp. Rotting. In a drawer he found a candle. No way to
light it. He put it in his pocket. He walked out into the

gray light and stood and he saw for a brief moment the
absolute truth of the world. The cold relentless circling of
the intestate earth. Darkness implacable. The blind dogs
of the sun in their running. The crushing black vacuum
of the universe. And somewhere two hunted animals
trembling like groundfoxes in their cover. Borrowed time
and borrowed world and borrowed eyes with which to
sorrow it. (*R* 110)

If following the catastrophic event and the subsequent birth
of the child the mother and father differ on the possibility of
sorrow, that is, I think, because they differ too on the possibility of hope, or on the hope of possibility. The father can
sorrow only in the light of hope's possibility, and he can hope
only in light of sorrow's: he sees, perhaps, the truth spoken
elsewhere in McCarthy that one "ought not let sorrow die for
it is the sweetening of every gift" (*Crossing* 288); the mother
cannot sorrow, she can neither receive the gift of a child nor
give herself to it, because she cannot hope, and this marks the
condition also of her love. And here, on the question of love,
the father and mother may diverge less than appears at first
glance. The mother chooses suicide and refuses sorrow, for she
sees no life or world; the father decides on survival and accepts
the sorrow that still reveals—if through "borrowed eyes" (*R*
110)—a possible world. Both, however, might be seen to have a
shared understanding of the essential interdependence between
a living, or possible, world and love. The mother believes that
they are not survivors but walking dead—because they have
no world within which to dwell with the open expectation that
love both demands and permits. If we are already dead, or if
death's presence has become all-consuming, then love proves
impossible, or meaningless, as does any further talk or any
story (and this is why the father is right to insist as he does that
death is not a lover). The father, by contrast, would hold the
same belief but differently: life and world are not possible if we
do not love, and the hope of life and world, whose appearance
is in fact always and only to borrowed eyes, rests in the child,
his heart, who—amidst the burned earth and its cold secular

winds—carries the fire, and passes the breath, of life. For both the father and the mother, love and possibility condition one another: a world without the openness of possibility (which is really no longer a world) makes the mother's love impossible; the father's love insists on the hope of possibility, which is to say of a world, in the child. . . .

. . . As I've been suggesting in my reading of *The Road*, a central figure of such openness, and of the co-implication between chance and danger, hope and sorrow, is the fragile and threatened child who may also be, as the story says, the word of God—one who, in this version, carries the fire, and passes the breath, of life in a dark and dying world. In *The Road*, this possibility—that the child is word of God—is just that: a possibility, which comes to light against the darkness of its potential negation. On the second page of the book, as the father watches "the ashen daylight congeal over the land," we learn that "He knew only that the child was his warrant. He [the father] said: If he [the child] is not the word of God God never spoke" (*R* 4). This possibility that God spoke, or that God now speaks through the child—for whom language and story and world and time might yet be possible or living—would have to be read here, I think, in light always of the possibility suggested by Ely (the only named character in the book), who contends later (in what I hear to be an echo of the mother's insistence that they are not survivors but walking dead), "There is no God and we are his prophets" (*R* 143). In *The Road*, as elsewhere, I'd say, the possibility of the one is conditioned by the possibility of the other—just as the possibility of life and world, time and language, require the possibility of a suspension, or a darkness, that illumines them.

Between the two, those on *The Road* might dwell, just as they might dwell, if minimally, between a memory and expectation whose interplay does not come to form a temporal image of the eternal present,[38] but rather keeps open the memory of a never fully realized expectation and the expectation of a memory that will never be completed. The father sees something of this on the verge of his death, where he cannot take the son—and this due not only to his inability or unwillingness "to hold

[his] dead son in [his] arms" (*R* 235), as he explains, but even more, I would say, due to the non-relational character of his Being-toward-death. The fact that his death—like the son's—remains non-transferable does not in any way compromise but indeed conditions and gives all of its force to the father's response, shortly before dying, to the son's objection "you said you wouldn't ever leave me": "I know," says the father, "I'm sorry. You have my whole heart" (*R* 235). Here, where neither one can step in for the other, the other has the heart of the one. And here, before the darkness, that worldly time is illumined in which, as happens toward the end, the father, "filthy, ragged, hopeless [would] stop and lean on the cart and the boy would go on and then stop and look back and he would raise his weeping eyes and see him standing there in the road looking back at him from some unimaginable future, glowing in that waste like a tabernacle" (*R* 230). In this worldly time, in the road, the father may well keep his promise to the son that he will not send the son into the darkness alone. And in that promise, which is spoken, at times, in religion and literature alike, we might hear the possible truth of the father's words that "all things of grace and beauty such that one holds them to one's heart have a common provenance in pain. Their birth in grief and ashes. So, he whispered to the sleeping boy. I have you" (*R* 46).

Notes

28. In this sense *The Road* carries to its extreme a movement operative also throughout other of McCarthy's works—especially *Blood Meridian* and the Border Trilogy—where the illumination of world most often occurs through forms of violent transition and transformation, interruption and event, decline and disappearance. The dream and the journey, the crossing and the catastrophe, the wounding and the blinding, the barely formed or long abandoned dwelling place, the ruin and the remnant: by means of these and related figures and themes McCarthy's work attends recurrently to forms of suspension and darkness that illuminate the world-hood of our worlds, highlighting both the fragile and the excessive possibility of life in the world, along with the deep negativity that conditions such possibility—as that which gives possibility by marking its absolute limit.

29. See along these lines the tale of the blinded revolutionary in *The Crossing*.

30. Recall the epigraph to *Blood Meridian* (New York: Vintage International, 1992) from Jacob Boehme: "It is not to be thought that the life of darkness is sunk in misery and lost as if in sorrowing. There is no sorrowing. For sorrow is a thing that is swallowed up in death, and death and dying are the very life of the darkness."

31. "Even now some part of him wished they'd never found this refuge. Some part of him always wished it to be over" (*R* 130).

32. Or, as the work later prompts one to ask (*R* 142), how does wishing one had died differ from wishing one had never been born?

33. For a powerful treatment of these questions within a reading of Vico and Heidegger, see Robert Harrison's *Dominion of the Dead*.

34. Though I will not here develop the point directly, it is worth noting, in the subsequent lines of this passage—"The sweeping waste, hydroptic and coldly secular. The silence" (*R* 231—that the "secular" in *The Road* (as elsewhere) may well be associated not with the worldly but with its collapse.

35. Such interplay between hope and sorrow would have to be understood also as the matter of a beauty both achieved by and meditated on within McCarthy's writing:

> He was beginning to think that death was finally upon them and that they should find some place to hide where they would not be found. There were times when he sat watching the boy sleep that he would begin to sob uncontrollably but it wasn't about death. He wasn't sure what it was about but he thought it was about beauty or about goodness. Things that he no longer had any way to think about at all. (*R* 109)

38. See especially Books X and XI of *The Confessions* for Augustine's influential treatment of memory, expectation and time in relation to the eternal present.

Works Cited

Augustine, Saint. *Augustine: Confessions*. Ed. James J. O'Donnell. Oxford: Oxford UP, 1992.

———. *Confessions*. Trans. R.S. Pine-Coffin. New York: Penguin Books, 1961.

———. *Tractates on the First Epistle of John. The Fathers of the Church: Saint Augustine, Tractates on the Gospel of John 112–21, Tractates on the First Epistle of John*. Trans. John Rettig. Washington: The Catholic U of America P, 1995.

Heidegger, Martin. *Being and Time*. Trans. John Macquarrie and Edward Robinson. Oxford: Basil Blackwell, 1962.

———. "Brief über den 'Humanismus'." *Wegmarken*. Frankfurt am Main: Vittorio Klostermann, 1967. 145–94.

———. *The Fundamental Concepts of Metaphysics: World, Finitude, Solitude*. Trans. William McNeill and Nicholas Walker. Bloomington: Indiana UP, 1995.

———. *Die Grundbegriffe der Metaphysik: Welt–Endlichkeit–Einsamkeit*. *Gesamtausgabe* Vol. 29/30. Frankfurt am Main: Vittorio Klostermann, 1983.

———. *Grundprobleme der Phänomenologie (1919/20)*. *Gesamtausgabe* Vol. 58. Frankfurt am Main: Vittorio Klostermann, 1993.

———. "Letter on Humanism." *Basic Writings*. Rev and expanded ed. Ed. David Krell. San Francisco: HarperCollins, 1993. 213–66.

———. *Phänomenologie des religiösen Lebens*. *Gesamtausgabe* Vol. 60. Frankfurt am Main: Vittorio Klostermann, 1995.

———. *The Phenomenology of Religious Life*. Trans. Matthias Fritsch and Jennifer Anna Gosetti-Ferencei. Bloomington: Indiana UP, 2004.

———. *Sein und Zeit*. Sechzehnte Auflage. Tübingen: Max Niemeyer Verlag, 1986.

McCarthy, Cormac. *The Crossing*. New York: Vintage Books, 1994.

———. *The Road*. New York: Alfred A. Knopf, 2006.

Migne, J.P. *Patrologiae Cursus Completus, Series Latina* Vol. 35. Paris: 1844–64.

CARL JAMES GRINDLEY ON THE NOVEL'S SETTING

There has been some debate regarding the setting of Cormac McCarthy's 2006 novel, *The Road*. If the book is read, however, as a document of the so-called Tribulation of Judeo-Christian mythology, many interpretive issues become readily resolved.

Questions regarding the novel's setting arise primarily because of the absence of a clear cause for the world's devastation. Although he does not mention it explicitly, McCarthy fills the novel with apocalyptic imagery. On one hand, the novel details neither nuclear weapons nor radiation, but the physical landscape, with its thick blanket of ash; the father's mystery illness; and the changes in the weather patterns of the southern United States all suggest that the world is gripped by something similar to a nuclear winter. On the other hand, the novel echoes many of the themes that John the Divine describes in the Book of Revelation—themes that would become the trademarks of nuclear winter. In particular, McCarthy's description of the novel's landscape aligns with the effects of the Seven Seals (Rev. 6.1–6.17), Seven Trumpets (8.6–9.21), Seven Thunders (10.1–10.7), and Seven Vials (16.1–16.21). The effects seen in Revelation and *The Road* include fire from heaven, the trees and the grass burned up, ships destroyed, all sea life dead, the sun and the moon blotted out, plagues and earthquakes, cities full of unburied dead people, and so on. Although similarities between McCarthy's descriptions and Revelation provide more than enough clues to argue for a supernatural cause, there are a few other pieces of evidence.

First, there is the father's recollection of the event coming at 1:17 (time of day unspecified), when there was a "shear of light and a series of low concussions" (52). I believe this time to be an allusion to Revelation 1.17, which introduces Christ's theophany to John the Divine: "And when I saw him, I fell at his feet as dead. And he laid his right hand upon me, saying unto me, Fear not; I am the first and the last." Following his appearance, John then receives knowledge of the eschaton. In the context of the novel, if the event that caused the destruction of the earth was supernatural in origin, then much is explained: inconsistencies between descriptions of burned people and burned buildings (in *The Road*, the wilderness and people are burned, but structures are mostly intact), strange earthquakes (very rare in the southeastern United States), dead seas, dead rivers, dead oceans, strange weather, the missing sun and moon, and so on. Likewise, the recurring images of pilgrimage and millennial cults become more meaningful.

Second, McCarthy's language is rich in religious, primarily Christian terminology. On one hand, apart from a large supply of Judeo-Christian lexical items (e.g., *God*, thirty-three times and *Christ*, five times), McCarthy's lexicon in *The Road* features several unique items, including his only published uses of *Christendom*, *creedless*, *ensepulchred*, *enshroud*, and *godspoke*, and some relatively rare items, including *tabernacle* and *chalice*. On the other hand, the novel does not contain any lexical items relating to atomic warfare, nor does McCarthy use forms of disaster or catastrophe or other related words to describe the novel's central event (Sepich and Forbis).

Third, it could be argued that the dream of the beast on the novel's first page is an allusion to the conclusion of Yeats's "Second Coming." Such an allusion would hardly be out of the ordinary for McCarthy—after all, he wrote a book called *No Country for Old Men*. Likewise, McCarthy has approached biblical topics in his other works, the most obvious being the title of *Cities of the Plain*.

Once the novel's setting is proposed, then some of its episodes take on greater weight. For example, the encounter with the man struck by lightning takes on more impact as an obvious allusion to St. Paul. Likewise, the father and son's encounter with Ely (161–75) turns into an encounter with the prophet Elijah. Even the mother's bleak assessment, first dismissing the idea that they are "survivors" (55) and then asserting that her "only hope is for eternal nothingness and [she] hope[s] it with all [her] heart" (57), turns into a very real choice of oblivion over the torment of hell because she has missed the Rapture.

Tellingly, therefore, if the novel takes place post-Rapture, the father's characterization of his son: "If he is not the word of God God never spoke" (5) points to the father's need for his son as a religious need. The son is the father's personal savior, but, in many ways, the father also serves as his Christ's protector. In this regard, *The Road* is the anti-*Adekah*—the story of a faithless father who refuses to sacrifice his son on an altar built to his own atheism.

Finally, the child's unspecified age becomes more important, because according to standard Christian interpretations of Daniel's prophecy of seventy weeks (Dan. 9.22–27), the tribulation described in Revelation is only supposed to last seven years. It could be that the father missed the second coming of Christ by moments.

Works Cited

The Bible. Ed. David Norton. London: Penguin, 2006.

McCarthy, Cormac. *The Road.* New York: Vintage, 2006.

Sepich, John, and Christopher Forbis. "A Concordance for *The Road.*" *Resources and Criticism Regarding the Novels of Cormac McCarthy.* 19 Nov. 2007 <http://www.johnsepich.com/a_concordance_to_the_road.pdf>.

ALEX HUNT AND MARTIN M. JACOBSEN
ON THE IMAGE OF THE SUN

Cormac McCarthy's Pulitzer Prize–winning 2006 novel *The Road* contains numerous allusions to the classical trope of light and the sun, notable in Plato's *Republic* as symbolic of wisdom, truth, and hope. In articulating his theory of forms, Plato's sun represents "the good," a concept that stands for an ideal pattern for an object and/or an absolute truth, such as justice, which our perceptual ability only glimpses. The imagery of light and darkness throughout *The Road* recalls Plato's "Simile of the Sun" (bk. 6, sec. 508) while particular details allude to what is perhaps the most influential story of the human faith in enlightenment, Plato's "Allegory of the Cave" (bk. 7, sec. 514). In referencing and revising Plato's allegory, McCarthy sets the scene for a central theme of the novel, the power and fragility of language in enabling meaning and thus civilization.

The "Simile of the Sun" expresses the concept of absolute reality as Socrates explains to Glaucon (Plato's brother) the fundamental need for illumination beyond human perception. He argues that the eye only sees what the sun illuminates, and thus, that the sun symbolizes reality whereas the eye is a symbol for an always contingent human perception. As Socrates says, we find that our intelligence comes "when the mind's eye is fixed on objects illuminated by truth." Conversely, when "fixed on the twilight world of change and decay" we "can only form opinions," our "vision confused and its opinions shifting." He concludes, "what gives the objects of knowledge their truth and the knower's mind the power of knowing is the form of the good. It is cause of knowledge and truth . . ." (308–09). This conceptualization is reversed in *The Road*. From the first page, we learn that light and truth are fading. We learn that the world of *The Road* lacks not only valid human perception but, even more disturbingly, the greater truth that makes it possible.

The novel begins as the man awakens from a dream in a dark wood. In this postapocalyptic ruin, even the days are "gray," as the air is filled with ash, suggesting the scenario of nuclear winter: "Nights dark beyond darkness and the days more gray each one than what had gone before. Like the onset of some cold glaucoma dimming away the world" (3). The man "looked toward the east for any light but there was none" (3). He then remembers his dream, in which "he had wandered in a cave where the child led him by the hand. Their light playing over the wet flowstone walls." They reach a "black and ancient lake" where they see "on the far shore a creature that raised its dripping mouth from the rimstone pool and stared into the light with eyes dead white and sightless" (3). The creature is "pale and naked and translucent, its alabaster bones cast up in shadow on the rocks behind it" (3); it "swung its head from side to side and then gave out a low moan and turned and lurched away and loped soundlessly into the dark" (4). The man does not question the dream, but for the reader it is a disturbing opening in its perverse references to Plato's allegory.

The dream of the cave, the imagery of light and dark therein, and the reference to glaucoma allude to Plato's "Allegory of the Cave," in which the concept of progressive illumination emerges through the story of prisoners chained in a cave and allowed only to see shadows. The name of Socrates' interlocutor, "Glaucon," and the term "glaucoma" descend from the Greek *glaukos*, the English equivalent of "glaucous." One sense of this terra is a grayish-blue dark color suggestive of the darkening earth of *The Road*; the medical condition glaucoma, which brings deteriorating vision and eventual blindness, also suggests darkening, blackness. In Plato's allegory, the character Glaucon is foil to the wise Socrates, and Glaucon's coming to understand the concept of progressive illumination is the metaphor for progressive illumination.

In *The Road* we have the inverse situation, the world becoming steadily colder and darker as human wisdom is lost. Rather than being liberated by the discovery of the sun, the pallid cave-dwelling creature runs from the light. Although the boy leads the man through the cave and they do bear a light, it is by no means a hopeful dream. McCarthy's allegory of the cave is not about getting out to the sun and to illuminating wisdom but about going in deeper, lost in the darkness with a fading light.

In attempting to create a system of meaning to sustain his son and himself, reassuring the boy that they are "carrying the fire" (71), the man recognizes in the loss of language the fragility of meaning: "The names of things slowly following those things into oblivion. Colors. The names of birds. Things to eat. Finally the names of things one believed to be true. More fragile than he would have thought. How much was gone already? The sacred idiom shorn of its referents and so of its reality" (75). Rather than a higher reality of Platonic forms, in McCarthy's account the loss of the physical form exposes the contingency of the idea—an inversion of Platonic thinking. In another passage that suggests the passing of Platonic idealism, he holds his son, tousles his hair, thinking "All of this like some ancient anointing. So be it. Evoke the forms. Where you've nothing else construct ceremonies out of the air and breathe upon them" (63).

Understanding McCarthy's allusion to Plato's allegory in the opening of the novel suggests an understanding of the novel's ending, as well, for the dream of the cave comes back to the man as he lies, barely conscious, dying: "Drip of water. A fading light. Old dreams encroached upon the waking world. The dripping was in the cave. The light was a candle which the boy bore in a ringstick of beaten copper. . . . In that cold corridor they had reached the point of no return which was measured from the first solely by the light they carried with them" (235–36). Soon after, the man assures his son, terrified at the father's imminent death, that "Goodness will find the little boy. It always has. It will again" (236). Yet understanding the anti-Platonic symbolism of the dream, the father's words ring hollow. That the boy meets a band of friendly people who take him in is a tenuous sort of happy ending, at best. The "point of no return" in the cave, the finite light from the candle, and the frame created by opening and closing with a glaucous, anti-Platonic objective correlative, bespeak an end to civilization, not its rebirth. The boy survives his father, but ultimately there will be no one to carry the fire.

BARBARA BENNETT ON THE IMAGE OF FIRE AND REFERENCES TO YEATS'S POETRY

True to Cormac McCarthy's roots, his latest book *The Road* (and to some degree, his previous novel *No Country for Old Men*) is replete with Celtic influences and allusions to one of Ireland's favorite poets, W. B. Yeats. The title of *No Country*, of course, is a quotation from Yeats' "Sailing to Byzantium" and works in a thematic sense as a prequel to *The Road*. In the final paragraph of *No Country*, Sheriff Bell recounts a dream he had of his father, riding on horseback through a cold and snowy pass in the mountains. As his father passes him. Bell sees that "he was carrying fire in the horn" and knew that his father was "goin on ahead and that he was fixin to make a fire somewhere out there in all that dark and all that cold" (309). In this final section, Bell also recounts the story of a man who, in the midst of an unsettled wilderness, "set down with a hammer and chisel and carved out a stone water trough to last ten thousand years." Bell wonders at the "faith" this man shows, believing it was "some sort of promise in his heart" for future generations—a promise Bell feels he himself could not make (308–9).

The phrase from Bell's dream, "carrying the fire," is a significant refrain in *The Road*, spoken between the unnamed father and son. Most reviewers have generally agreed that the "fire" is hope, spiritual belief, or truth, but a closer understanding of Celtic tradition reveals what McCarthy more likely meant. In the Celtic culture, the hearth fire was the center of family activity, providing warmth, light, and food for the family.

Another writer with Appalachian roots, Ron Rash, describes the significance of the hearth fire in his novel, *Saints at the River*: "A family's hearth fire was never allowed to die down completely. . . . When children left to marry and raise their own families, they took fire from their parents' hearth with them. It was both heirloom and talisman, nurtured and protected because generations recognized it for what it was—living memory" (111).

McCarthy's father worked for the Tennessee Valley Authority and would have been privy to the legends surrounding these transplanted hearth fires. In the TVA Association newsletter of September 2007, for example, a former worker on the TVA retells the story about a Tennessee farmer who refused to leave his home, despite a "superior house" awaiting him. "When engineers pushed him for a reason, the 'old man' said his father asked him to promise he would never let the fire go out on the hearth because his grandfather had lit the fire when the cabin was built." Eventually the engineers figured out a way to move the fire without letting it go out, and the man relented, saying, "'I only wanted to keep the fires of my forefathers alive'" (5).

As "living memory" the fire is the place where family storytelling took place, a place to pass down family tales and lineages orally. In *The Road*, too, storytelling plays a significant role. McCarthy writes that the father "told the boy stories" around the fire at night: "Old stories of courage and justice as he remembered them" (41). He is passing on the stories of their now-decimated society—their "living memory" of a time when the world still held acts of courage and justice. The father remembers when there were always "books and papers," but then recalls when "he'd stood in the charred ruins of a library where blackened books lay in pools of water. Shelves tipped over. Some rage at the lies arranged in their thousands row on row" (187). Unlike the "faith" of the stone carver in *No Country*, the destroyer of the library lacked the belief that there will ever be a future where once again stories of "courage and justice" will be truth, not lies.

The boy resists his father's tales, saying they "are not true." Instead, he wants stories that could be true in his current day, stories in which they help other people, not avoid them. His father reminds him that he has "stories inside" that haven't been told yet. These, his father implies, are what the boy will pass along in addition to the stories his father has told him, continuing to "carry the fire" that the boy finally realizes is within himself (268–9).

The Celtic references begin in *The Road* on the first page in a dream the father has about a creature "who raised its dripping mouth from the rimstone pool and stared into the light with eyes dead and sightless as the eggs of spiders" (3–4). When added to references McCarthy makes to "tattered gods slouching in their rags across the waste" (52) and travelers "slouching along with clubs in their hands" (60), it seems clear McCarthy is alluding to Yeats' often-quoted poem, "The Second Coming" in which a beast with "lion body and the head of a man" with a "gaze blank and pitiless as the sun" "slouches towards Bethlehem to be born."

Like Yeats, McCarthy does not envision the Second Coming as a joyful return of Jesus Christ, but rather wonders what monster might appear to take payment for our destructiveness and greed. So many of the "good" characters in McCarthy's novel—like the wife and mother of the traveling pair who had committed suicide rather than continuing to live in a seemingly hopeless world—"lack all conviction," while those on the road who are willing to do whatever it takes to survive—including torture, murder, and cannibalism—seem full of the "passionate intensity" of the evil in Yeats' poem.

And in a final nod to Yeats, the ultimate paragraph of *The Road* describing brook trout brings to mind the "salmon-falls, the mackerel-crowded seas" in "Sailing to Byzantium." In both places the fish are remnants of the old world, the "maps and mazes" of memory and of a "thing which could not be put back" (287), in a place where old men could still survive, as opposed to this new world which must be inhabited by a different kind of being. The father in *The Road*, just like Sheriff Bell in *No Country for Old Men*, can no longer survive in this post-apocalyptic landscape and must die before the next generation can accomplish its destiny, whatever that may be.

In *The Road*, Cormac McCarthy's post-apocalyptic tale of a father and son traveling in the aftermath of the world's collapse, we are thrust into a land of remains. The land is barren and covered in ashes. The sky is dark, and everything is dry. For those unfamiliar with the book, there is no intricate plot in *The Road*. The plot is sparse, as is the dialogue. The man and boy walk, hunt for scraps of food, speak in short sentences, and navigate around any signs of human life. Moving south in hopes of escaping the onset of winter, they make their way around a road, a place of passage but also a place of danger. Each encounter invokes dread and suspicion. All those who remain are potential competitors for the meager supplies—gas, blankets, and jars of preserves. McCarthy maps the landscape of survival, describing it in desolate terms such as "cauterized terrain," "dull sun," and "ashen scabland" (12, 13).

McCarthy tells us very little about what brought about the end of the world. "The clocks stopped at 1:17 pm. A long shear of light and a series of low concussions" (45). He offers us glimpses of the previous world through the father's memories. We know that the mother committed suicide, choosing not to go on in a world that no longer exists. The son, born before the collapse, knows no other world than this one. Throughout the novel, man and boy, both unnamed, move through the remains, of houses, of streets, of dried-out streams and barren farmlands. Two bullets remain in the father's gun over the course of their journey. Death is inevitable, if not welcomed. As they find their way to the warmer climate, it becomes increasingly clear that the father, whose health is declining throughout, will be unable to continue.

The last several pages narrate the farewell between father and son. The boy encounters a family who, the reader infers, takes in the boy now that his father has died. In the penultimate paragraph, the woman embraces the boy. McCarthy writes:

> She would talk to him sometimes about God. He tried to talk to God but the best thing was to talk to his father and

he did talk to him and he didn't forget. The woman said that was all right. She said that the breath of God was his breath yet though it pass from man to man through all of time. (241)

Without reading the book, the reader might sense the possibility of hope, of divine presence, even of redemption. Although the father has died, the son will live on and carry on the father's memory. We can, perhaps, heave a sigh of relief and breathe again. But those who have made it through the 240 pages of *The Road* may have a more complicated reaction to these final paragraphs. In McCarthy's post-apocalyptic world, people have resorted to cannibalism in order to survive. The images of a child on a spit and burnt flesh cannot easily be erased as we think of the future of the boy without his father.

Reviews of the book diverge greatly in their reading of the final two paragraphs. Does McCarthy provide, in the end, a picture of redemption? Does the boy's survival—a survival beyond the death of the father—constitute a redemptive ending? Some find the notion of a redemptive ending sentimental, unrealistic, and inconsistent with the rest of the book and its unrelenting picture of doom. For them, McCarthy resorts to a picture of redemption, redeeming a world that can no longer be redeemed. Others interpret the boy's survival as a testimony to the persistence of hope and regeneration, a necessary ending to the tender father–son relationship that McCarthy presents. For them, McCarthy is depicting the substance of hope and the triumph of parental love in the face of terror.

The debate about redemption is not new in McCarthy interpretation. In assessing *Blood Meridian*, Dana Phillips points to two camps of interpretation: the "southern" and the "western." Reading McCarthy as a southern writer, the images and language of redemption are central; he is interpreted along the trajectory of William Faulkner and Flannery O'Connor, who draw on Christian themes—in many cases, to launch strong critiques of them. Reading him as a western writer, nihilistic images prevail. His landscapes and characters are Nietzschean, and violence obliterates any redemptive framework.

The shift from the early southern setting of Tennessee to the southwestern states (from *Orchard Keeper* to *The Crossing*, for example) prompts philosophical—and theological—questions. In *The Road*, McCarthy returns to the South. From what we can discern, this is post-apocalyptic Tennessee. This return "home" for McCarthy enters him back into the familiar frameworks of religious vocabulary; probing the question of a redemptive ending is, in this sense, warranted. Yet he does so after passing through the western territories, in which he interrogates American identity and its redemptive mythology. Robert Brinkmeyer describes the landscape in McCarthy's western novels as the "geography of terror" (38).[1] Speaking about *Blood Meridian*, Charles McGrath says that McCarthy's novels "describe a world that is, for all intents and purposes, either prehistoric or post-apocalyptic: a barren, hostile place in which civilization—and any recognizable notion of morality—is scarcely discernible" (qtd. in Brinkmeyer 39–40). McGrath's statement predates The Road, yet it is clear with this novel that the post-apocalyptic has arrived in McCarthy's writing. Here, there are only traces of a past civilization.[2]

The quest that McCarthy sends us on in *The Road* is one in which temporal markers of past, present, and future no longer hold. At the beginning of the novel, the man wakes up in the night, and we are immediately told that there is no distinction between night and day. All, it seems, is an eternal middle; there is nothing to anticipate, and the past is what haunts the father, reminding him of a world he can never get back. McCarthy catches the reader in a schizophrenic, and distinctively American, post-apocalyptic crisis of meaning: between the craving for a happy ending (for resolution, for redemption) and the recognition of its impossibility (there is, in Christian terms, no resurrection ahead).

In this article, I claim that this haunted, post-world territory cannot simply be interpreted within a redemptive framework. By this I mean that the question of a redemptive ending is not the question that McCarthy presents to us in *The Road*. Instead, he confronts us with the question of the aftermath: what does it mean to witness to what remains? Key components of the redemptive paradigm are employed by the father, but the reader is pressed to think, *towards what end?* The biblical imagery and religious allusions cannot be simply placed or interpreted within a traditional framework of redemption. The language of redemption is exposed, not in order to reveal its violence or to claim its fulfillment, but as a remnant of an irrecoverable world.[3]. . .

. . .The story of America is not an innocent one. In his novels, McCarthy narrates this repeatedly. Naming violence for "what it is" is a central message of the western novels. Florence Stricker describes *Blood Meridian* as follows: "All that remains is America, *just as it is* (Baudrillard), with no sacred mission, no manifest destiny, no chosen people, no promised land: a scene without any sign" (159). McCarthy has explicitly exposed the dark side of the American redemption narrative in his novels. Dana Phillips writes: "Salvation history, which understands the natural world and man's travails in it as symbols of the spirit, has long since been played out, as the ruined, eroded, and vulture-draped mission churches in *Blood Meridian* suggest" (34).

Yet, in *The Road*, the question of redemption returns, with allusions to biblical prophets and to the boy as a messianic figure. Three paragraphs into the book, McCarthy conveys the father's thoughts: "Then he just sat there holding his binoculars and watching the ashen daylight congeal over the land. He knew only that the child was his warrant. He said: if he is not the word of God God never spoke" (4). The question, however, is: how are we to interpret this language within the context of a world that has collapsed? The context is critical here. How do we read images such as the breath of God and the messianic references to the boy *after the end of the world?* This is a persisting and unavoidable dilemma for readers of *The Road*—the moment you think redemption, you encounter its impossibility—*the* ending has already happened.

Reading McCarthy through the lens of [Daniel] McAdams's [notion of the] redemptive self, we can see the template of American redemption in the interactions between the father and son. Throughout the novel, the father attempts to construct a meaningful world for the son. He draws on two aspects of the redemptive framework: identity and mission. The elements of identity and mission are conveyed through the statements, repeated throughout: "Are we the good guys?" and "We're carrying the fire." In the first, the son frequently asks his father for assurance of their identity as "good guys." This is often coupled with the opposite: the identification of others that they encounter as the "bad guys." The father has designated the world in this way in order for the boy to assess their actions and encounters accordingly. Their identification as "good" explains, and even justifies, actions that may otherwise be questionable. The pathos lies in the fact that this moral structure no longer makes sense in this post-apocalyptic world. The boy first asks: "Are we still the good guys?" following an incident in which the father kills a man. At several pivotal points, the boy returns to this question with, we might interpret, growing awareness that good and bad can no longer be distinguished.

The second, "We're carrying the fire," is a statement of mission. Through this statement, the father has given their journey purpose. The implication is that someone is waiting to receive the fire that they bear. Traveling over the dull and ashen ground, the father counters the monotony of the landscape by ascribing a higher meaning to their travels. Michael Chabon writes: "As they travel the father feeds his son a story, the nearest that he can come to a creed or a reason to keep on going: that he and his son are 'carrying the fire'" (24–25). It makes their existence necessary in a world in which necessity takes on its rawest form.

There is a terrifying scene in which they encounter a group of survivors huddled in a cellar. From the half burned body of one man, it is clear that they are staying alive by eating human flesh. The father and son do not talk about this encounter immediately, but after a short time, the son asks his father about it. "We won't ever eat anybody, will we?" The father assures him that they will not:

No. We wouldn't.
No matter what?

No. No matter what.
Because we're the good guys.
Yes.
And we're carrying the fire.
And we're carrying the fire. Yes.
Okay. (108–09)

In face of the ultimate terror—cannibalism—the father pre-serves a vision of the world as good and meaningful in the absence of both. Note that the term "okay" is constantly repeated in the novel. It is clear that things are not okay, but it is a word that holds together the world that the father has con-structed for the boy.

These statements comprise the boy's vocabulary for making sense of the world, and he continues to use them, even apart from his father's verbal reassurance. They appear in the closing pages. When he encounters the family in the moments after his father's death, he asks the man: "Are you carrying the fire?" The man replies: "Am I what?" "Carrying the fire," says the boy. "You're kind of weirded out, aren't you?" But the boy persists. "So are you?" The man answers: "Yeah. We are" (238–39). While these words are significant in creating a world for the boy, they do not, in the end, translate more broadly. Like the repetition of the word okay, they are, in Chabon's words, "like a sore place or a missing tooth" (25).

If we read this according to the template of American redemption, the boy's spirit will rise above the devastation, representing the promise of resurrection in the aftermath of death's finality. We grasp onto any sliver of hope. If anything, goodness will prevail. When the son asks about the fate of a little boy that they had met in their earlier travels, the father says: "Goodness will find the little boy. It always has. It will again" (236). Readers, thus, may take these statements and interpret them in line with a redemptive reading. The father provides a way of viewing the world that will sustain the boy as he outlives his father. The memory of the father will live on in the boy; he will transcend his suffering and move ahead into a more promising future.

Yet McCarthy does not offer this so cleanly. His final paragraph suggests that this world, whose "becoming" was once mapped on the backs of brook trout, cannot be repaired. He writes: "Maps and mazes. Of a thing which could not be put back. Not be made right again" (241). The destruction is full and unrelenting in the book, and it is difficult, if not impossible, to conceive of restoration. These two sentences—"We're the good guys," "We're carrying the fire"—can support a redemptive reading. But they can also unsettle redemption in the dissonance between their meaning and the reality into which they are spoken. Highlighting this dissonance seems to be consistent with the broader works of McCarthy, where, for example, in *Blood Meridian*, he raises basic questions about human nature and morality within the context of scalp-hunting. One of the things he is most effective at doing is denying his readers comfort, which he does by staging moral conversations in the most immoral places.

"Not be made right again." Does McCarthy waver on this statement? Is it retracted in his final line about the hum of mystery?[9] In review after review, the question is whether McCarthy delivers us from this devastating world. Either there is redemption or there is not. Into which camp does he ultimately place us—in the southern or in the western? I want to claim that this either/or is not the right framework for the world in which McCarthy places us. The line between good and bad and life and death dissolves in the territory of survival. A dissonance emerges when we map an either/or framework onto it. . . .

Trauma

. . . McAdams implies that, in the face of horrific suffering, the redemptive narrative is not only insufficient, but dangerous. He proposes a tragic framework as an alternative to a redemptive one. But it is not tragedy that we encounter in *The Road*. It is, instead, trauma.[13] Novelist John Burnham Schwartz comments: "[In *The Road*], the threat is not just dying; it's surviving."[14] I want to examine McCarthy's ending through the lens of trauma, or trauma theory. This interpretive lens unearths a different question than a redemptive one: What does it mean to be one who remains? Between the two McCarthy "camps," a third arises. In a post-world, can we think beyond redemption? . . .

. . . The "cauterized terrain" of *The Road* is one in which those living cannot find safety in anything around them and memories serve to haunt rather than to comfort. Concepts of progress and the future dangle as cruel impossibilities. The man and the boy journey in a traumatic landscape, living on in a world in which sense, meaning, and trust have been destroyed. The only thing that remains is their connection. According to a redemptive framework, this father–son connection is what is redemptive—a father's love triumphs.[19] This is not a theistic concept of redemption, but rather a picture of human redemption (i.e., "We save each other"). But, again, this triumph and hope shudders in the face of the statement: "Not be made right again."

A traumatic reading takes this statement—this "not be made right again"—as a starting point for interpretation. To think about the ending through a traumatic lens does not deny the tenderness between the father and the son and the power of human connection in the face of peril; but it does take away, in Wood's words, the redemptive gloss. How can we read these final pages *without* retracting the radical and irreparable end that McCarthy has presented throughout? This question is not a defeatist one; neither is it one that calls for the mere opposite of a triumphant redemptive narrative. Instead, it addresses the dissonance between the context and interpretive framework. In this tension, a different orientation to life in the aftermath of death arises. . . .

. . . [Michael] Chabon suggests, in his review of *The Road*, that McCarthy takes his readers on a "harrowing" journey through the underworld. He likens the novel to other epic adventures in which heroes pass through hell. The father, like Odysseus and Aeneas, is haunted by the ghosts of his past and be and the son are "daily obliged to harrow" the gray sunless hell (26).[28] Chabon's reference to the "harrowing of hell" clearly invokes redemption; it, he claims, "is the father's greatest preoccupation." Chabon reminds us again of the dissonance between the father's mission and the landscape of remains: " . . . in the face of the bleakness and brutality of their lives his mission is difficult to sustain" (25). Pursuing an alternative account of the descent may address this dissonance, invoking not a vocabulary of redemption but, instead, a vocabulary of survival and witness.

The arrival of the man and woman at the end of the novel does not provide relief. How do we know, even in the end, that the boy will be safe? McCarthy has led us to mistrust all encounters throughout *The Road*. This arrival does not ensure redemption; instead, it throws the reader again into the tenuous territory of remaining: When trust and meaning are shattered, what remains? When there is no promise of life ahead, what remains? These are the questions that the American redemptive template overlooks, or, in Wood's words, glosses. When Chabon describes the journey between father and son as a "harrowing of hell"—an underground account brought above ground—I suggest that we counter it with another reading. It is not a harrowing journey but, instead, one that places readers between death and life as witnesses to the impossibility of things "being made right again." Recovering this middle moment in the redemption narrative provides a testimony to what cannot be made right, what cannot be recovered.

To think theologically after the collapse is not to garner the redemptive narrative in the face of terror. Instead, it means receiving the statement "Not be made right again," not as the nihilistic foil to the redemption narrative, but as an imperative to witness to what remains when all constructs for making meaning have been shattered. Reading *The Road* within a redemptive framework eclipses this imperative to witness, closing the text that should, instead, be "handed over" to its readers with the perilous question: What does it mean to witness to what remains?

Conclusion

Though McCarthy presents us with a stunning picture of what it means to be one who remains, his reviewers lead us, in the end, to a simpler question than his context demands: is there redemption or not? McCarthy's post-apocalyptic setting, however, pushes us onto different soil. And the redemptive compass proves ineffective. Reading his context in light of trauma theory, the redemptive identity and mission provided by the father is forced, highlighting the dissonance between reality and interpretation. Drawing on the insights of Wood, I interpret this dissonance as a weakness in McCarthy's theology. His context demands a different theological framework than the one he provides. I have suggested, if only briefly, that a rereading of the Christian narrative of the descent into hell could disrupt the American narrative of redemption, providing, instead, a rich vocabulary for thinking about a more mixed relationship between death and life.

It is not a triumph over death that one faces in *The Road* but, instead, a testament to the ways in which life and death can no longer be distinguished. This "crisis of survival" reveals not only the insufficiency of many traditional theological explanations but also unearths a different genre of writing that is organic to theology, that of testimony and witness. In the aftermath of the collapse of the world, there is no end in sight, no destination, and no promise of life ahead. But in the face of these impossibilities, the impulse to impose redemption is replaced, instead, by an imperative to witness to what remains. Could we discover, in these texts, a witnessing breath, not a triumphant one?[29] Instead of leading to a redemptive ending, it may provide a necessary disruption of that familiar framework and a reorientation to life as a *living on*. As readers, we are handed over the perilous question: "What does it mean to witness to what remains?" The question is not who will save the world but, instead, who will witness its shattering?

Notes

1. Brinkmeyer writes: "McCarthy explores the violent origins of westward expansion that have been expunged from the national mythology that celebrates the victory of civilization over savagery and the march of progress driving, and justifying, America's manifest destiny" (38).

2. Throughout *Blood Meridian*, McCarthy demonstrates that human nature, from its very origins, is violent. Brinkmeyer points us to an epigraph in *Blood Meridian* from the *Yuma Daily Sun* in which

"a 300,000-year-old fossil . . . shows evidence of being scalped." Brinkmeyer comments that the significance of this epigraph for the novel is clear: "violence lies at the heart of humankind; it always has, it always will" (39). This presents a stunning contrast to the father's words at the end of *The Road*: "Goodness will find the little boy. It always has. It will again" (236). McCarthy's characters in the West, Brinkmeyer says, are often "described as creatures from primitive, if not prehistoric, times; they are manifestations of our forebears, humanity in its original state" (29). Is McCarthy changing what he understands to be elemental about human nature? Has violence (West) turned into goodness (return to the South)?

3. Brinkmeyer, in writing about *Blood Meridian*, also warns against the danger in interpreting the biblical references too simplistically. "There appears, moreover, little hope for religious salvation amidst all the destruction, despite the numerous biblical references that dot the novel. But these dots never connect, never coalesce into a pattern either for understanding the bleak and incomprehensible void or for transcending it" (43).

9. The last four sentences of the book read: "Maps and mazes. Of a thing which could not be put back. Not be made right again. In the deep glens where they lived all things were older than man and they hummed of mystery" (241).

13. McAdams claims that in tragic narratives, suffering is not necessarily redeemed but, rather, endured. "The tragic hero learns that suffering is an essential part of life, even when the suffering has no ultimate meaning, benefit, or human cause." He writes: "Tragedy gives fuller expression to the ambivalence and the complexity of human lives than do many other narrative forms. It looks with skepticism upon the kind of ideological certitude celebrated in the redemptive self" (266). Trauma, however, reveals a different relationship to suffering. In tragedy, there is a moral purpose at work, a process of education. The assumption of a certain moral ordering is still in place. This cannot be assumed in trauma. It's not just enduring something but, rather, waking us to its shattering. It is a radical rupture of a moral ordering of the world. See Sands 41–61.

14. Likewise, in *Unclaimed Experience*, Caruth queries: "Is trauma the encounter with death, or the ongoing experience of having survived it?" (7). At the core of these stories, I could suggest, is thus a kind of double telling, the oscillation between a crisis of death and a correlative crisis of life: between the story of the unbearable nature of an event and the story of the unbearable nature of its survival.

19. The father, early on in the novel, claimed that the son is the only sign of God that he can recognize. At the end, the son implies that the father operates as a god. "He tried to talk to God but the best

thing was to talk to his father and he did talk to him and he didn't forget" (241). The divine status attributed to each, at either end of this novel, could be read as an allusion to the Father–Son relationship in the gospel accounts and, most strikingly, to the Johannine gospel narrative. In that gospel, the concepts of mission, memory, and sacrifice are central to the divine narrative of Father and Son, and they are often interpreted in terms of redemptive love.

28. Chabon writes: "The world post-apocalypse is not Waterworld; it's the Underworld. In his stories, his memories, and above all in his dreams, the father in *The Road* is visited as poignantly and dreadfully as Odysseus or Aeneas by ghosts, by the gibbering shades of the former world that populate the gray sunless hell which he and his son are daily obliged to harrow" (26).

29. I return to the end of McCarthy's *The Road* in order to rethink the "breath of God," which he refers to in the final paragraphs of the book.

Works Cited

Brinkmeyer, Robert H., Jr. *Remapping Southern Literature: Contemporary Southern Writers and the West*. Athens: U of Georgia P, 2000.

Brison, Susan J. *Aftermath: Violence and the Remaking of a Self*. Princeton: Princeton UP, 2002.

Brueggemann, Walter. "Readings from the Day 'In Between.'" *A Shadow of Glory: Reading the New Testament after the Holocaust*. Ed. Tod Linafelt. New York: Routledge, 2002. 105–15.

Caruth, Cathy, ed. *Trauma: Explorations in Memory*. Baltimore: Johns Hopkins UP, 1995.

———. "Parting Words: Trauma, Silence and Survival." *Cultural Values* 5 (2001): 7–27.

———. *Unclaimed Experience: Trauma, Narrative, and History*. Baltimore: Johns Hopkins UP, 1996.

Caruth, Cathy, and Deborah Esch, eds. *Critical Encounters: Reference and Responsibility in Deconstructive Writing*. New Brunswick: Rutgers UP, 1995.

Chabon, Michael. "After the Apocalypse" Rev. of *The Road*, by Cormac McCarthy. *The New York Review of Books* Feb. 2007: 24–26.

Derrida, Jacques. "Living On: Border Lines." Trans. James Hulbert. Harold Bloom, Paul De Man, Jacques Derrida, Geoffrey H. Hartman, and J. Hillis Miller. *Deconstruction and Criticism*. New York: Continuum, 1979. 75–176.

———. *Sovereignties in Question: The Poetics of Paul Celan*. Ed. Thomas Dutoit and Outi Pasanen. New York: Fordham UP, 2005.

Felman, Shoshana, and Dori Laub. *Testimony: Crisis of Witnessing in Literature, Psychoanalysis, and History*. New York: Routledge, 1991

Graef, Ortwin de, Vivian Liska, and Katrien Vloeberghs. "Introduction: The Instance of Trauma." *European Journal of English Studies* 7 (2003): 247–255.

Hall, Wade, and Rich Wallach, eds. *Sacred Violence: A Reader's Companion to Cormac McCarthy*. El Paso: Texas Western, 1995.

Herman, Judith. *Trauma and Recovery*. New York: Basic, 1997.

Kennedy, William. "Left Behind." Rev. of *The Road*, by Cormac McCarthy. *New York Times Book Review* 8 Oct. 2006: 1+.

Korn, Martin L. "Trauma and PTSD: Aftermaths of the WTC Disaster—An Interview with Bessel A. van der Kolk, MD." *Medscape General Medicine* 3.4 (October 2001). 15 Jul. 2009 <http://www.medscape.com/viewarticle/408691>.

Langewiesche, W. "American Ground: Unbuilding the World Trade Center. *Atlantic Monthly* July–Aug. 2002: 45–79.

Levine, Peter A. *Healing Trauma: Restoring the Wisdom of Your Body*. Louisville, CO: Sounds True, 2008.

McAdams, Daniel. *The Redemptive Self: Stories Americans Live By*. New York: Oxford UP, 2006.

McCarthy, Cormac. *The Road*. New York: Knopf, 1996.

Mirarchi, Steven A. *Faith of the Unbelievers: Contemporary American Fiction Questions God*. Diss. Brandeis U, 2002.

Parrish, Tim. "The Killer Wears the Halo: Cormac McCarthy, Flannery O'Connor, and the American Religion." *Sacred Violence: A Reader's Companion to Cormac McCarthy*. Ed. Wade Hall and Rick Wallach. El Paso: Texas Western, 1995. 25–39.

Phillips, Dana. "History and the Ugly Facts of *Blood Meridian*." *Cormac McCarthy: New Directions*. Ed. James D. Lilley. Albuquerque: U of New Mexico, 2002. 17–46.

Sands, Kathleen. "Tragedy, Theology, and Feminism in the Time After Time." *New Literary History* 35 (2004): 41–61.

Scarry, Elaine. *The Body in Pain: The Making and Unmaking of the World*. New York: Oxford UP, 1985.

Schwartz, John Burnham. MP3 Commentary. "The Audio Book Club on Cormac McCarthy." 31 May 2007. *Slate*. 28 Feb. 2008 <http://www.slate.com/id/2167335/>.

Stricker, Florence. "'This New Yet Unapproachable America': (For) An Ethical Reading of Cormac McCarthy's Western Novels." *Cormac McCarthy: Uncharted Territories*. Ed. Christine Chollier. Reims, France: UP of Reims, 2003. 147–61.

Wood, James. "Getting to the End." Rev. of *The Road*, by Cormac McCarthy. *New Republic* 21 May 2007: 44–48.

Woodward, Richard B. "Cormac McCarthy's Venomous Fiction." *New York Times Magazine*. 19 Apr. 1992. *New York Times on the Web*. 1997. New York Times Company. 10 Mar. 2008 <http://www.nytimes.com/books/98/05/17specials/mccarthy-venom.html>.

ASHLEY KUNSA ON STYLE IN *THE ROAD*

Cormac McCarthy's Pulitzer Prize–winning tenth novel *The Road* (2006) gives us a vision of *after*: after the world has come to disaster, after any tangible social order has been destroyed by fire or hunger or despair. McCarthy here surrenders his mythologizing of the past, envisioning instead a post-apocalyptic future in which human existence has been reduced to the basics.[1] Though the book remains silent on the exact nature of the disaster that befell the planet some ten years prior, the grim results are clear. No plants grow, no sun shines through the ash-plagued sky and, save a single dog, no animals survive. The dead outnumber the living in shocking proportion, and of those few living humans, most are barely human at all: they are "men who would eat your children in front of your eyes," members of "bloodcults" bearing lead pipes and marching with chained slaves and catamites in tow (*The Road* 152, 14).[2] The protagonists—an unnamed man and his young son—push a shopping cart across the wasted earth, freezing, starving and threatened at every turn, in search of the sea and in hope of a warmer, more hospitable place. Given the horrific devastation, we are not surprised that language also has been returned to its rudiments and now must be re-imagined. This task is well-suited to McCarthy, who since the early days of *The Orchard Keeper* (1965) has demonstrated considerable stylistic facility and flexibility. Yet critics have generally shown little interest in McCarthy's style, preferring instead to "talk about what he's talking about" (Ellis 157).[3]

Scholarly debate over what McCarthy is talking about has often focused on the issue of meaning versus meaninglessness. In *The Achievement of Cormac McCarthy*, Vereen M. Bell lays out the view of McCarthy as nihilist, identifying in the author's first six novels little by way of plot, theme or character self-consciousness and motivation.[4] For Bell, these missing elements amount to "McCarthy's metaphysic summarized: none, in effect—no first principles, no foundational truth" (*Achievement* 9).[5] Maiming, killing and the defiling of corpses, on the other hand, figure prominently in the novels, and this "violence tends to be just that; it is not a sign or symbol of something else" (Phillips 435). The emphasis on violence notwithstanding, Edwin T. Arnold challenges the popular nihilist thesis, asserting that there is "always the possibility of grace and redemption even in the darkest of his tales," though such redemption requires more of McCarthy's characters than they seem capable of giving ("Naming" 46). . . . But while grace and redemption are at best tenuous, unrealized possibilities in prior McCarthy novels, in *The Road* these aspects fundamentally drive the narrative: out of love for his child and hope for some salvation, the man pushes himself to the point of death to preserve the child's physical and spiritual safety. . . .

. . . The style of *The Road*, on the contrary, is pared down, elemental, a triumph over the dead echoes of the abyss and, alternately, over relentless ironic gesturing. And it is precisely in *The Road*'s language that we discover the seeds of the work's unexpectedly optimistic worldview. The novel, I argue, is best understood as a linguistic journey toward redemption, a search for meaning and pattern in a seemingly meaningless world—a search that, astonishingly, succeeds. Specifically, I demonstrate how McCarthy's odd approach to naming establishes the conditions for a New Earth, a New Eden.[10] In the redemption of language, *The Road* suggests, we discover the hope for our redemption. . . .

. . . In the world of *The Road*, basic differences divide the good from the bad. As with the novel's other characters, the man and child lack proper names, but prior to the novel's advent, the father has given the two a collective designation that highlights their underlying nature: he and the boy are the "good guys" who, Prometheus-like, are "carrying the fire" as they search for other "good guys" (*TR* 70). Their status as good guys inheres in, if nothing else, their refusal to eat people or dogs. This is fact enough to separate them from the "bad guys": cannibals who feast on human cattle chained in a basement or those responsible for "a charred human infant headless and gutted and blackening on the spit" (78, 167).[11] In fact, some years before the novel's opening, the boy's mother committed suicide in fear of falling prey to such atrocities. The father ponders a similar fate not a few times, but he does not acquiesce to suicide's lure; rather, he honors his responsibility. "My job is to take care of you," he tells the child, "I was appointed to do that by God. I will kill anyone who touches you" (65). Although the father commits acts that, by our present standards, if not immoral and unethical, are at least reprehensible, he does these things solely for the safety of the child.[12] And early on, the pair's journey acquires an explicitly religious quality, a sense of divine mission reinforced by the antonomastic refrain of "good guys"—that is, the substituting of this phrase for their proper names—and the repetition of "carrying the fire," phrases that become incantatory in the manner of a litany or a prayer.

This religious quality extends to the novel's overall approach to character naming, which demonstrates a search for the prelapsarian eloquence lost in the postlapsarian babble. This is a search not simply for the original names given the world by Adam, but also, more fundamentally, for the God-given capacity to name the world correctly. The novel's treatment of its only "properly" named character, the nearly blind old traveler who calls himself "Ely," illustrates this negotiation with language.[13] "Ely what?" asks the father, to which the old man responds, "What's wrong with Ely?" (*TR* 141). His reticence about offering personal information is immediately clear and is underscored when the father asks his age and "what line of work" he's in (144). "I'm not anything," Ely insists (145). *Outer Dark*'s bone-chilling gang leader says, "They say people in hell ain't got names. But they had to be called somethin to get sent there" (235–36),[14] and if we liken *The Road*'s burned earth to hell, we must recognize the man's efforts at naming Ely as attempts to find a way out of hell, a search for and belief in an alternative. When pressed about his name, the old man ultimately admits that "Ely" is a lie, saying of his real name, "I couldnt trust you with it. To do something with it. I dont want anybody talking about me. To say where I was or what I said when I was there. I mean, you could talk about me maybe. But nobody could say that it was me. I could be anybody" (*TR* 144–45). Without a "real" name, Ely cannot be held responsible for his words and deeds. He is, in essence, un-tethered, wandering the road beholden to no one and nothing, and thus escaping punishment (whether God's or that of another man on the road, we are never sure). But ultimately, the narrative rejects the lie that is "Ely"—the idea that a person can invent a convenient identity to hide who he is and what he has done. All that the father knows for sure of this stranger is that he is an "old man"; hence this is the most accurate and truthful thing to call him and the name that the narrative relies on. . . .

. . . Free as it is of proper names, *The Road* often relies on pronouns for character identification. Short by nature, pronouns allow McCarthy to emphasize the characters' deeds by drawing away as little attention as possible from action verbs, as is evident in the following passage, in which the man and boy engage a knife-wielding marauder:

> He was a big man but he was very quick. He dove and grabbed the boy and rolled and came up holding him against his chest with the knife at his throat. The man had already dropped to the ground and he swung with him and leveled the pistol and fired from a two-handed position balanced on both knees at a distance of six feet. The man fell back instantly and lay with blood bubbling from the hole in his forehead. The boy was lying in his lap with no expression on his face at all. He shoved the pistol in his belt and slung the knapsack over his shoulder and picked up the boy and turned him around and lifted him over his head and set him on his shoulders and set off up the old roadway at a dead run, holding the boy's knees, the boy clutching his forehead, covered with gore and mute as a stone. (*TR* 56)

The focus here is on action—"dove," "grabbed," "rolled," "dropped," "swung," "leveled," "fired," "fell," "shoved," "slung," "lifted"—and the passage's style demands that we judge a man, that we know him, by the nature of his deeds, not by the name he is called. We must read who he is, determine his inherent goodness or vileness, by the actions he commits with regard to other men. It is simple and essential. Furthermore, the confusion we might first feel (or at least expect) about pronouns and agency, about who is doing what, is subverted because the characters' actions make clear who they are. In this single dramatic instance, for example, the character to whom the pronouns "he," "him," and "his" refer switches some twelve times, nine of the pronouns lack grammatically correct antecedents, and the phrase "The man" that begins consecutive sentences refers in the first to the father and in the second to the "roadrat." Despite this, the characters are clearly knowable and differentiable from one another by what they *do*. And, in a world where ethical and moral distinctions matter, they can be taken to task for what they do, at least by the reader, if not by some authority within the text.

The pronouns in *Blood Meridian* at times seem purposely to lack clarity, suggesting the interchangeability of actors and actions, but, while *The Road* favors pronouns more heavily than *Blood Meridian* or any other McCarthy work, its pronouns are very clear and correspond to the sharp difference between good and evil. That McCarthy has identified this distinction suggests a hopeful turn in his fiction: if the characters (and the reader) can draw the line between right and wrong, then that which is right and good can be identified with, championed and possibly attained. Even Chabon, who reads the main characters' journey as essentially futile, concedes that "we are rooting for them, pulling for them, from the first—and so, we suspect, is the author" (117). Indeed, the reader has greater access to the father's thoughts than to those of any other McCarthy character, and as a result he is rounder, fuller and more sympathetic. He is someone the reader can imagine chatting with every morning before work at the bus stop, were this a world with jobs and bus stops. The failure of the father's lungs at *The Road*'s end is heartrending, and his death is made bearable only because the great sacrifice of his labored journey secures for the child a hopeful future. Though the sea is neither warm nor blue as the child had dreamed, he is found by a family of four, the new "good guys," and with them he can continue to carry the fire. . . .

. . . Despite obvious similarities among the settings, however, McCarthy's stylistic presentation of *The Road* differs significantly from that of his previous works.[16] Specifically, the narrative offers very few proper place names, and of the handful contained in the book, none is a marker of the story's action.[17] To the question of where the characters are located, then, reviewer Tom Chiarella answers, "There's no way to know. The names of cities have been forgotten" (94). But the text does not bear out this assertion. The man demonstrates considerable familiarity with the locales through which he and the boy pass, and the boy "had the names of towns and rivers by heart" (*TR* 181). And McCarthy, who always "carefully charts his characters' movements from street to street or town to town—you can follow them on maps if you wish" (Arnold, "Blood and Grace" 11), has just as meticulously crafted this pair's journey: the man and boy do follow an "oil-company roadmap"—in pieces and numbered by crayon, but a map nonetheless (*TR* 36). The narrative's strategy is actually one of withholding place names, a provocative rhetorical move that forces the reader to imagine new possibilities, to think not solely in terms of the world that was, but also of the world that will be. The burned out landscape, strangely, is a new if unlikely Eden awaiting once again those perfect names.

In simplest terms, the proper place names of the pre-apocalyptic world have become obsolete. The world of *The Road* lacks organized governments, religions and economies, essential social structures that we readers take for granted, and thus is bereft of those classifications that would help to place the characters in the physical sense: country, state, county, city. Pointing at the map, the man explains to the boy,

These are our roads, the black lines on the map. The state roads
Why are they the state roads?
Because they used to belong to the states. What used to be called the states.
But there's not any more states?
No. (*TR* 36)

The man's addendum—"What used to be called the states"—
points to the names' lack of relevance in the novel's present.
The states are no longer states, so calling the roads "state
roads" is merely a throwback, and a term that, of course,
means nothing to the child who was not yet alive during the
time of the past civilization. To read this strategy as a nihilistic voiding of the places in the world as the reader knows it,
though, would be a mistake. Rather, as the past world itself
becomes meaningless, *The Road* suggests, the names of the past
become meaningless as well. This is not to say that meaning
has gone out of the world. The point here is that the nature
of the meaning has changed: the method of naming McCarthy
uses offers a refiguring of meaning in the language of the new,
post-apocalyptic world.

This meaning inheres in the very human elements of the
world. As such, the style here is distinctly hopeful for its focus
on the good guys' survival. For what matter is the distinction
between Tennessee and Georgia, or, for that matter, between
Tennessee and Timbuktu, in a world devoid of the social
structures that give meaning and function to the distinctions?
The number of miles between points A and B, one's location
with regard to a body of potable water—these are the important matters of geography in McCarthy's "feverland" (*TR* 24).
For example, the man "thought they had enough food to get
through the mountains but there was no way to tell. The pass
at the watershed was five thousand feet and it was going to be
very cold" (25). Here, place is calculated by the characters and
related to the reader in terms of food and warmth. Descriptions
such as this one convey information of vital importance to the
characters on their journey, information that helps them to get
their bearings and ultimately to survive. At another point the
man "sat crosslegged in the leaves at the crest of a ridge and
glassed the valley below them with the binoculars. The still
poured shape of a river. The dark brick stacks of a mill. Slate
roofs. An old wooden watertower bound with iron hoops. No
smoke, no movement of life" (66). These details are essential
for assessing danger: the starving pair need to enter the city to
search for food, and while still-standing buildings and a river

could suggest the presence of dangerous people, the lack of smoke and movement indicates otherwise.

Omitting the names of the pre-apocalyptic world allows the ruined places (and the ruined civilization of which they were a part) to be left in the past. . . .

. . . But where is *The Road*'s road? Using the narrative's place descriptions and their similarities to real places in McCarthy's earlier works, Chabon, Wesley G. Morgan and others have placed the action in the southeastern U.S.[18] The novel returns to the fictional terrain of McCarthy's first four books, all of which are set in the American southeast. The setting's physical return to the site of McCarthy's earliest works all the more strengthens the meaning of the author's stylistic departure in representing this setting. The physical return signals a return to the beginning, to a time before all was tarnished and destroyed, a time characterized by potential. Finding a new way to talk about this now-destroyed region implies the possibility of renewal. The old might become new again, once more meaningful and pure, in a new world with a new language that can make it so.

By divesting the post-apocalyptic landscape of those names that signify the now ruined world, *The Road* frees both character and reader from the chains of the old language. Eliminating the old suggests the coming of the new and creates a space in which the new world can be imagined and called into being. The slate, of course, has not been entirely cleaned; the corpses of the old world, both literal and figurative, are everywhere. The world posed by McCarthy's novel exists at a decidedly proto-Edenic moment: it is still in the stages of becoming, with regard to both form and content. But this world's very existence in the face of such unlikely odds is itself the hopeful suggestion of an alternative to stark existential nothingness. The fact that the characters refuse to fall back on the old methods of naming demonstrates their belief in a better way to name and a better world of which to speak, even if they (and the novel) have not yet found these things. Just as something optimistic propels the characters through the ashen landscape—a hope for warmth, for safety, for more good guys—the optimistic naming scheme propels the reader to imagine other possibilities. . . .

. . . That the earth on which the characters trek is yet properly unnamed tells the reader that neither the man nor the narrator is the Adam who will give a new language to the new Eden. Each is of the old, pre-apocalyptic world; each began his story there, came into language there and failed there. But the boy is different. Born several days after the apocalyptic "long shear of light" and "series of low concussions," he is decidedly of the new world (*TR* 45). The boy serves as an Adamic figure, a messiah not unlike Christ himself, who "must struggle on, so that he can be present at, or somehow contribute to, the eventual rebirth of the world" (Chabon 112). Indeed, the father and son's decade-long survival in the face of such brutal and unlikely odds is "providential," their tale "a messianic parable, with man and boy walking prophetically by rivers, in caves, on mountaintops and across the wilderness in the spiritual spoor of biblical prophets" (Kennedy 11). In decidedly biblical language, the narrative early on alerts the reader to the child's holy nature: "If he is not the word of God God never spoke" (*TR* 4), thinks the man, even as he often disbelieves in and curses God. After washing the dead man's brains from the boy's hair, the man muses, "All of this like some ancient anointing," and "Golden chalice, good to house a god" (63, 64). Even in dialogue the man suggests outright that the boy is holy, asking Ely, "What if I said that he's a god?" (145). Further, as the man is dying, he calls the child "the best guy" (235), a superlative that elevates the boy above simple "good guy" status and sets him apart from his father and any other decent human beings. . . .

. . . *The Road*'s moment of supreme clarity regarding the child's true nature, by contrast, comes in two simple sentences. When the father tells the child, "You're not the one who has to worry about everything," the child responds, "Yes I am . . . I am the one" (*TR* 218). This moment shines not simply for its transparency, but also for its singularity and the change it suggests: here, the boy unequivocally states who he is, whereas previously he has looked to his father for answers, asking whether they are the good guys. The certainty and clarity with which the boy for the first time puts his own words to himself contribute to the statement's decidedly messianic ring. This line is reminiscent both of John 14:6, where Jesus proclaims, "I am the way, the truth, and the life," and of Matthew 16:15, where Jesus prods his disciples by asking, "But whom say ye that I am?" Unlike the judge, the god of war, the boy promises mercy and redemption. His proclamation follows the discovery of the thief who stole their food, shoes and blankets, when the father has said, "I'm going to leave you the way you left us," and divested the man of all clothing and property (*TR* 217). The child, distraught over this eye-for-an-eye mentality, begs his father to show the man mercy and forgives the unrepentant thief without a thought.

By naming himself "the one," the boy here, only a few days before his father's death, bears out the idea that he is, indeed, the one for whom the world is waiting. And already he has not only named himself, but also provided another character with the closest thing to a "real" name in *The Road*. Throughout the novel the child calls his father "Papa";[22] this is the only word of its kind used as a form of address, a fact that underscores the essential nature of the father–son relationship that guides every moment of the novel's action.[23] This relationship has survived—in fact, it enables survival after the world has come to such a terrible state—and "the strength of it helps raise the novel—despite considerable gore—above nihilistic horror" (Zipp 14). The choice of such an affectionate term, moreover, as opposed to a more formal word such as "Father," highlights the deep, intimate nature of the pair's relationship. When the man who finds the boy after the father's death asks, "Was that your father?" the boy's response is a confirmation, but also a correction that reaffirms the boy's ability to name that bond: "Yes. He was my papa" (*TR* 237). And the child's burgeoning ability to name—to say simply and directly what a thing is and, like Adam, to make it so—is made more powerful by his ability to read and write,[24] even in the absence of a culture that supports and nurtures these activities. Together, these abilities suggest that he can go forward, beyond the novel's end, to write the new story of the new world. . . .

. . . McCarthy uncharacteristically writes possibility into the ending of *The Road* by giving the child a fighting chance. Five pages before the story's close, the man, now wounded by an arrow, his lungs nearly failing, says his final words to the child: "Goodness will find the little boy. It always has. It will again" (*TR* 236). In the night the man dies, leaving his son alone and starving on the road. And after three days, goodness—much as it does in the Gospels—does, in fact, arrive: the child is found by another traveler, the father of a young boy and girl. These new "good guys" (they don't eat people either) welcome the child among them, and in the next-to-last scene, the man's wife tells the boy "that the breath of God was his breath yet though it pass from man to man through all of time," strengthening the Adamic connection and recalling Genesis. McCarthy emphasizes this link in a closing scene that tells how "Once there were brook trout in the streams in the mountains. . . . In the deep glens where they lived all things were older than man and they hummed of mystery" (241). The end and the beginning are inseparable in *The Road*. For it is the end of the old world that signals the possibility of a new one, and the novel's own ending so clearly harkens back to a beginning, the beginning of time. . . .

. . . We cannot traverse *The Road* without a startling awareness of its departure from McCarthy's previous style. Along with its odd approach to naming, the fractured narrative structure, proliferation of sentence fragments, and brief, repetitive dialogue differentiate the novel from the rest of his work. Doubtless, some critics will charge that in *The Road* McCarthy is not "McCarthy" enough: that, by alluding to some possibility beyond our present (and the novel's future) world, he sentimentalizes the horrible facts of our collective situation. These critics will precisely miss the point. It is one thing to render on the page a dreadful world so intensely that the reader cannot contest its veracity, and of this trade, McCarthy has long been master practitioner. But it is another thing altogether—and this, the far more difficult—to render a dreadful world while simultaneously conjuring an alternative with such clearness of vision that its truth is likewise unquestionable. This McCarthy does in *The Road* without flinching. . . . The novel veers away from the "paradigm of a dead-end, paradigmless world" (Bell, "Ambiguous Nihilism" 32), away from the void, signaling a radically optimistic shift for one of contemporary fiction's most celebrated and prolific authors.

More broadly, *The Road* is an argument for a new kind of fiction, one that survives after the current paradigm of excess collapses, after the endlessly witty posturing exhausts itself with its own self-reflective neuroses. I am not arguing that the "postmodern" is dead. Those arguments have long been made, spoiled, and made again. And McCarthy's place in the post-modern canon (likewise, in that of the modernists) has been and will continue to be debated—by others.[26] What is evident, how-ever, is McCarthy's refusal to accept the postmodern condition. Further, his answer is most assuredly not the often celebrated but seldom well-defined "posthumanism"—*The Road* is too optimistic and too biblical. However difficult to fathom on the novel's hellish earth, the main characters are the "good guys," and this they are because they hold fast to those rigidly human qualities that the novel posits we are very much not "post": love, hope, courage. Just as these basic forms hold together what remains of this ruined fictional world, McCarthy searches for the essential elements of story—character, meaningful action, etc.— that hold narration together when artifice, self-consciousness and irony are burned away. Chabon is wrong in claiming that "the quest here feels random, empty at its core" (117). The "maps and mazes" at *The Road's* end point toward something essential at the center of the journey, and tellingly, the novel closes not with the intersection of arbitrary and nonsensical lines, but with the patterns on the backs of the trout, "maps of the world in its becoming," forms that suggest an inherent order and underlying purpose yet undiscovered (241). . . .

. . . In *The Road*, McCarthy has granted us this new Pro-metheus, a twenty-first-century good guy, Adam reinvented: the child is carrying the fire of hope and righteousness from the old story toward the new one. The father gives his son language, and after the father's death, the son goes on to seek that still elusive New Jerusalem that waits somewhere beyond the pages of the novel. Decidedly, *The Road* is not a *tabula rasa*, not a re-imagining from scratch; it takes what remains after the world has been destroyed and goes forward from there in search of what is next. And what we have in the novel's style is the post-apocalyptic language of a simultaneously new and age-old work: a means of looking forward, to after, by seeking the basic forms again. The paradoxical achievement of McCarthy's novel is that it accepts the disjunction between where the world/fiction has been and where it is going, and in this moment of possibility—after the old and before the new— reconciles barbarous destruction with eloquent hope.

Notes

1. McCarthy is best known for *Blood Meridian* (1985), which begins around 1850 and extends into the late nineteenth century, and the novels of The Border Trilogy (1992–1998), which are set in the 1950s. *No Country for Old Men* (2005) takes place in 1980, the most recent time period in McCarthy's previous work.

2. Hereafter, in-text references to *The Road* and *Blood Meridian* will be abbreviated *TR* and *BM*, respectively.

3. Since the beginning of his career, McCarthy has been unable to escape stylistic comparisons with other authors, most frequently Faulkner, Hemingway, Melville, and Flannery O'Connor. Often cited is Prescott's review of *The Orchard Keeper*, which deems McCarthy "Still Another Disciple of William Faulkner." Still, few in the wide body of McCarthy scholarship go beyond cursory comparisons, and even fewer take the author's style as a primary subject. Notable exceptions include Bingham, Kreml, Trotignon, and Ellis. The first three authors' studies investigate a stylistic aspect of their respective novels as a means of illuminating some particular aspect of the work, while Ellis traces the development of the sound of McCarthy's language from *The Orchard Keeper* through *The Crossing*. The present study differs from these earlier efforts in that it conducts a stylistic analysis of *The Road* in order to read the novel as a whole.

4. For other critics who take up and extend the nihilism thesis, see, for example, Ditsky and Winchell.

5. Prior to his book-length work, Bell investigated some of these ideas in "The Ambiguous Nihilism of Cormac McCarthy."

10. Arnold, in "Naming, Knowing, and Nothingness: McCarthy's Moral Parables," argues that McCarthy's early novels, up to and including *All the Pretty Horses* (1992), demonstrate "a profound belief in the need for moral order" (46), and he connects various key themes with the books of Matthew, I Corinthians and Revelation. While Arnold's ideas here and elsewhere have certainly laid the groundwork for arguments against claims of nihilism, it should be noted that he

does not contend that the novels develop the concept and underscore the existence of redemption—as does the present article with regard to *The Road*—but simply that the novels' worlds are not entirely devoid of moral possibility.

11. When confronted with this image, Swift's "A Modest Proposal," minus the irony, comes quickly to mind. Perhaps we should also think of Gulliver, although unlike Swift's character, the man in *The Road* does not give himself over to misanthropy as his travel story unfolds.

12. The father, for example, kills a man who attempts to kill the boy; runs away from a basement full of human captives to save his son's life; refuses food to a number of fellow travelers on the road; and, when he finds the man who has stolen his and the boy's clothes and supplies, forces the thief to strip down and leaves him empty-handed, as the thief had left them. All of this, however, is done in his role as the boy's protector, not for the man's own benefit, and he never harms anyone out of malice.

13. The name "Ely" paired with the characters' discussion of God in this section, of course, conjures the biblical prophet Elijah, who will return to the earth on the Day of Judgment before the Messiah. The bedraggled character in *The Road* is also reminiscent of the "old disordered Mennonite" in *Blood Meridian* (39), whom Bloom views as parallel with the prophet who calls himself Elijah in Melville's *Moby Dick* (viii).

14. McCarthy's dialogue frequently represents dialects, and words such as "somethin" are deliberate departures from spelling conventions. Likewise, spelling oddities in *The Road*, such as "couldnt" and "dont" which appear in later examples in this article, are consistent stylistic features of the novel, not typesetting errors.

16. It likewise differs from the name-heavy antecedents of the modernist literary aesthetic, and specifically from T. S. Eliot's *The Waste Land*, the emblematic example of modern apocalyptic literature. Certainly *The Road*'s "ashes of the late world carried on the bleak and temporal winds to and fro in the void. Carried forth and scattered and carried forth again. Everything uncoupled from its shoring" (*TR* 9–10) recall "These fragments I have shored against my ruins" at the end of *The Waste Land*, not to mention the earlier "fear in a handful of dust." But in Eliot's poem, the cities of "falling towers"—Jerusalem, Athens, Alexandria, Vienna, London—are all named and, therefore, memorialized.

17. *The Road* contains six proper place names: Rock City, Tenerife, London, Cadiz, Bristol and Mars. The first comes in the form of a sprawling barn-side advertisement—"See Rock City" (*TR* 18)—and although this might initially promise to help identify a specific setting, literally hundreds of barns in the United States, from Michigan in

the north, to Texas in the west, bear this slogan. Hence this place name does little to narrow down the novel's location beyond what most readers will already be able to determine (see Note 18). The narrator's conjecture that a boat's iron hardware has been "smeltered in some bloomery in Cadiz or Bristol" (228) is likewise unhelpful for placing the action, as these could be towns, respectively, in Kentucky and Tennessee or Spain and England. Since, in a global economy, the location of an item's production hardly corresponds to its ultimate destination, "London" (192), written on a sextant the man finds on another ship, thus also fails to place the characters.

18. Some reviewers have proposed different locations. Kennedy, for example, asserts that the characters are traveling toward the Gulf Coast, while Abell says they are headed for the Pacific Ocean, and Weeks claims that the pair is in the American southwest, en route to California. The more common assertion that the characters are in Kentucky and Tennessee, on their way to the Atlantic Ocean, however, seems most supported by textual evidence. Morgan identifies present-day or past locations that correspond to some of the novel's descriptions, such as the Cumberland Gap, Knoxville and the Henley Street Bridge over the Tennessee River (originally of *Suttree* fame), and with these he reconstructs partially the main characters' route to the sea. Interestingly, Morgan sees this journey as corresponding to McCarthy "fictionally returning once again to his own roots in Knoxville and the southeast" (10).

22. For better or worse, one can't help but be reminded of Hemingway's nickname here, given the similarities between and numerous comparisons of Hemingway's and McCarthy's work (and, specifically, comparisons between Hemingway's style and the style of *The Road*).

23. While the "names" of the kid in *Blood Meridian* and the child in *The Road* share a common grammatical construction, I do not believe that McCarthy is establishing a parallel or connection between the characters or their functions. Eaton contends that the kid's "lack of a surname signals a certain rootlessness, and indeed the kid is cut off from his family from the start" (162). After leaving his father and home at the novel's opening, the kid is, by the second page of *Blood Meridian*, "finally divested of all that he has been. His origins are become remote" (*BM* 4). But the father-son bond in *The Road* is, of course, one of the work's strongest elements, and this relationship is sufficient to "root" the child by providing a sense of belonging. Further, the child's namelessness is consistent with that of all the other characters in the novel.

24. The kid in *Blood Meridian*, says Masters, "finally lacks the Adamic capacity to name and create, and his illiteracy . . . functions as a defining feature" (35). Thus he is unable to pose a real threat to the

all-consuming creative power of the judge, and he ultimately dies by the judge's hand.

26. For discussions of McCarthy as a postmodernist author, see, for example, Jarrett's *Cormac McCarthy*, chapter five, and "Cormac McCarthy's Sense of an Ending: Serialized Narrative and Revision in *Cities of the Plain*," and also Shaviro. For McCarthy as a modernist author, see Holloway and Horton. Phillips contends that McCarthy fits into neither of these categories, while Guinn outlines what he sees as McCarthy's development from a modernist to a postmodernist.

Works Cited

Abell, Stephen. "Another Terra Damnata." Rev. of *The Road*. *Times Literary Supplement* 10 Nov. 2006: 19–20. Print.

Arnold, Edwin T. "Blood and Grace: The Fiction of Cormac McCarthy." *Commonweal* 121.19 (1994): 11+. Print.

———. "Naming, Knowing and Nothingness: McCarthy's Moral Parables." Arnold and Luce 45–69.

Arnold, Edwin T., and Dianne C. Luce, eds. *Perspectives on Cormac McCarthy*. Rev. ed. Jackson: UP of Mississippi, 1999. Print.

Bell, Vereen M. *The Achievement of Cormac McCarthy*. Baton Rouge: Louisiana State UP, 1988. Print.

———. "The Ambiguous Nihilism of Cormac McCarthy." *Southern Literary Journal* 15.2 (1983): 31–41. Print.

Bingham, Arthur. "Syntactic Complexity and Iconicity in Cormac McCarthy's *Blood Meridian*." *Language and Literature* 20 (1995): 19–33. Print.

Bloom, Harold. Introduction. *Blood Meridian, or, The Evening Redness in the West*. New York: Modern Library, 2001. v–xiii. Print.

Boudway, Michael. "Christmas Critics." Rev. of *The Road*. *Commonweal*. 1 Dec. 2006: 19. Print.

Chabon, Michael. *Maps and Legends: Reading and Writing along the Borderlands*. San Francisco: McSweeney's, 2008. Print.

Charles, Ron. "Amid Fire and Torment." Rev. of *The Road*. *Washington Post* 1 Oct. 2006: T6. Print.

Cheuse, Alan. "Brilliant Writing Makes McCarthy's Dark Tale Shine." Rev. of *The Road*. *Chicago Tribune* 24 Sept. 2006: 5. Print.

Chiarella, Tom. "All the Pretty Horses Have Died." Rev. of *The Road*. *Esquire* Sept. 2006: 94–95. Print.

Daugherty, Leo. "Gravers False and True: *Blood Meridian* as Gnostic Tragedy." Arnold and Luce 159–74.

Ditsky, John. "Further into Darkness: The Novels of Cormac McCarthy." *Hollins Critic* 18.2 (1981): 1–11. Print.

Eaton, Mark A. "Dis(re)membered Bodies: Cormac McCarthy's Border Fiction." *Modern Fiction Studies* 49.1 (2003): 155–80. Print.

Eliot, T. S. *Collected Poems, 1909–1962*. London: Faber and Faber, 1963. Print.

Ellis, Jay. "McCarthy Music." Wallach 157–70.

Guillemin, George. "'See the Child': The Melancholy Subtext of *Blood Meridian*." Lilley 239–65.

Guinn, Matthew. "Ruder Forms Survive: Cormac McCarthy's Atavistic Vision." Wallach 108–15.

Helm, Michael. "McCarthy's Dark Road to Nowhere." Rev. of *The Road*. *Globe and Mail*. 7 Oct. 2006: D6. Print.

Holloway, David. *The Late Modernism of Cormac McCarthy*. Westport, CT: Greenwood, 2002. Print.

Horton, Matthew R. "'Hallucinated Recollections': Narrative as Spatialized Perception of History in *The Orchard Keeper*." Lilley 285–312.

Jarrett, Robert L. *Cormac McCarthy*. New York: Twayne, 1997. Print.

———. "Cormac McCarthy's Sense of an Ending: Serialized Narrative and Revision in *Cities of the Plain*." Lilley 313–42.

Kennedy, William. "Left Behind." Rev. of *The Road*. *New York Times Book Review*. 8 Oct. 2006: 1+. Print.

Kirves, Kyle. "Index of Character Names in the Novels." Wallach 303–85.

Kreml, Nancy. "Stylistic Variation and Cognitive Constraint in *All the Pretty Horses*." *Sacred Violence*. 2nd ed. Ed. Wade Hall and Rick Wallach. Vol. 2. El Paso: Texas Western, 2002. 37–49. Print.

Lewis, R. W. B. *The American Adam: Innocence, Tragedy, and Tradition in the Nineteenth Century*. Chicago: U of Chicago P, 1955. Print.

Lilley, James D., ed. *Cormac McCarthy: New Directions*. Albuquerque: U of New Mexico P, 2002. Print.

Masters, Joshua J. "'Witness to the Uttermost Edge of the World': Judge Holden's Textual Enterprise in Cormac McCarthy's *Blood Meridian*." *Critique* 40.1 (1998): 25–37. Print.

McCarthy, Cormac. *Blood Meridian, or, The Evening Redness in the West*. 1985. New York: Modern Library, 2001. Print.

———. *Child of God*. New York: Random House, 1973. Print.

———. *The Orchard Keeper*. New York: Random House, 1965. Print.

———. *Outer Dark*. New York: Random House, 1968. Print.

———. *The Road*. New York: Knopf, 2006. Print.

———. *Suttree*. New York: Random House, 1979. Print.

Morgan, Wesley G. "The Route and Roots of *The Road*." The Road Home: Cormac McCarthy's Imaginative Return to the South. University of Tennessee Conference Center, Knoxville, Tennessee. 26 April 2007. Paper. Knoxville: University of Tennessee Libraries, Newfound Press. Web. 16 Nov. 2008. <http://www.lib.utk.edu/newfoundpress/mccarthy/wesmorganarticle.pdf>. 1–11.

Owens, Barcley. *Cormac McCarthy's Western Novels.* Tucson: U of Arizona P, 2000. Print.

Phillips, Dana. "History and the Ugly Facts of Cormac McCarthy's *Blood Meridian.*" *American Literature* 68.2 (1996): 433–60. Print.

Prescott, Orville. "Still Another Disciple of William Faulkner." Rev. of *The Orchard Keeper. New York Times.* 12 May 1965: 45–46. Print.

Sepich, John Emil. "The Dance of History in Cormac McCarthy's *Blood Meridian.*" *Southern Literary Journal* 24.1 (1991): 16–31. Print.

———. *Notes on Blood Meridian.* Rev. and expanded ed. Austin: U of Texas P, 2008. Print.

———. "'What Kind of Indians Was Them?': Some Historical Sources in Cormac McCarthy's *Blood Meridian.*" *Southern Quarterly* 30.4 (1993): 93–110. Print.

Shaviro, Steven. "'The Very Life of the Darkness': A Reading of *Blood Meridian.*" Arnold and Luce 145–58.

Trotignon, Béatrice. "Detailing the Wor(l)d in *Suttree.*" Wallach 89–99.

Wallach, Rick, ed. *Myth, Legend, Dust: Critical Responses to Cormac McCarthy.* Manchester: Manchester UP, 2000. Print.

Weeks, Jerome. "After the Apocalypse." Rev. of *The Road. Dallas Morning News* 24 Sept. 2006: 7G. Print.

Winchell, Mark Royden. "Inner Dark: or, The Place of Cormac McCarthy." *Southern Review* 26.2 (1990): 293–309. Print.

Zipp, Yvonne. Rev. of *The Road. Christian Science Monitor* 3 Oct. 2006: 14. Print.

JOHN JURGENSEN ON THE BACKSTORY TO *THE ROAD*

The backstory of Mr. McCarthy's novel is deeply personal, springing from his relationship with his 11-year-old son, John, whom he had with his third wife, Jennifer. As death bears down in "The Road," the main character obsessively protects his son and prepares him to carry on alone: "He knew only that the child was his warrant. He said: If he is not the word of God God never spoke."

Mr. McCarthy flew here from his home near Santa Fe to visit the production office of his friend Tommy Lee Jones. A star of "No Country for Old Men," the actor directed and starred with Samuel L. Jackson in a film based on a play by

Mr. McCarthy, "The Sunset Limited." It begins with one man preventing another from hurling himself in front of a subway train, and will air on HBO. . . .

. . . Messrs. McCarthy and Hillcoat showed easy affability in their friendship, despite what could have been a prickly collaboration.

Mr. Hillcoat told him, "You relieved a huge burden from my shoulders when you said, 'Look, a novel's a novel and a film's a film, and they're very different.'"

In a soft voice, chuckling frequently and gazing intently with gray-green eyes, Mr. McCarthy talked about books vs. films, the apocalypse, fathers and sons, past and future projects, how he writes—and God.

The Wall Street Journal: When you sell the rights to your books, do the contracts give you some oversight over the screenplay, or is it out of your hands?

Cormac McCarthy: No, you sell it and you go home and go to bed. You don't embroil yourself in somebody else's project.

WSJ: When you first went to the film set, how did it compare with how you saw "The Road" in your head?

CM: I guess my notion of what was going on in "The Road" did not include 60 to 80 people and a bunch of cameras. [Director] Dick Pearce and I made a film in North Carolina about 30 years ago and I thought, "This is just hell. Who would do this?" Instead, I get up and have a cup of coffee and wander around and read a little bit, sit down and type a few words and look out the window.

WSJ: But is there something compelling about the collaborative process compared to the solitary job of writing?

CM: Yes, it would compel you to avoid it at all costs.

WSJ: When you discussed making "The Road" into a movie with John, did he press you on what had caused the disaster in the story?

CM: A lot of people ask me. I don't have an opinion. At the Santa Fe Institute I'm with scientists of all disciplines, and some of them in geology said it looked like a meteor to them. But it could be anything—volcanic activity or it could be nuclear war. It is not really important. The whole thing now is, what do you do? The last time the caldera in Yellowstone blew, the entire North American continent was under about a foot of ash. People who've gone diving in Yellowstone Lake say that there is a bulge in the floor that is now about 100 feet high and the whole thing is just sort of pulsing. From different people you get different answers, but it could go in another three to four thousand years or it could go on Thursday. No one knows.

WSJ: What kind of things make you worry?

CM: If you think about some of the things that are being talked about by thoughtful, intelligent scientists, you realize that in 100 years the human race won't even be recognizable. We may indeed be part machine and we may have computers implanted. It's more than theoretically possible to implant a chip in the brain that would contain all the information in all the libraries in the world. As people who have talked about this say, it's just a matter of figuring out the wiring. Now there's a problem you can take to bed with you at night.

WSJ: "The Road" is this love story between father and son, but they never say, "I love you."

CM: No. I didn't think that would add anything to the story at all. But a lot of the lines that are in there are verbatim conversations my son John and I had. I mean just that when I say that he's the co-author of the book. A lot of the things that the kid [in the book] says are things that John said. John said, "Papa, what would you do if I died?" I said, "I'd want to die, too," and he said, "So you could be with me?" I said, "Yes, so I could be with you." Just a conversation that two guys would have. . . .

WSJ: How does the notion of aging and death affect the work you do? Has it become more urgent?

CM: Your future gets shorter and you recognize that. In recent years, I have had no desire to do anything but work and be with [son] John. I hear people talking about going on a vacation or something and I think, what is that about? I have no desire to go on a trip. My perfect day is sitting in a room with some blank paper. That's heaven. That's gold and anything else is just a waste of time.

WSJ: How does that ticking clock affect your work? Does it make you want to write more shorter pieces, or to cap things with a large, all-encompassing work?

CM: I'm not interested in writing short stories. Anything that doesn't take years of your life and drive you to suicide hardly seems worth doing. . . .

WSJ: You were born in Rhode Island and grew up in Tennessee. Why did you end up in the Southwest?

CM: I ended up in the Southwest because I knew that nobody had ever written about it. Besides Coca-Cola, the other thing that is universally known is cowboys and Indians. You can go to a mountain village in Mongolia and they'll know about cowboys. But nobody had taken it seriously, not in 200 years. I thought, here's a good subject. And it was.

WSJ: You grew up Irish Catholic.

CM: I did, a bit. It wasn't a big issue. We went to church on Sunday. I don't even remember religion ever even being discussed.

WSJ: Is the God that you grew up with in church every Sunday the same God that the man in "The Road" questions and curses?

CM: It may be. I have a great sympathy for the spiritual view of life, and I think that it's meaningful. But am I a spiritual person? I would like to be. Not that I am thinking about some afterlife that I want to go to, but just in terms of being a better person. I have friends at the Institute. They're just really bright guys who do really difficult work solving difficult problems, who say, "It's really more important to be good than it is to be smart." And I agree it is more important to be good than it is to be smart. That is all I can offer you.

WSJ: Because "The Road" is so personal, did you have any hesitations about seeing it adapted?

CM: No. I've seen John's film ["The Proposition"] and I knew him somewhat by reputation and I thought he'd probably do a good job in respect to the material. Also, my agent [Amanda Urban], she's just the best. She wasn't going to sell the book to somebody unless she had some confidence in what they would do with it. It's not just a matter of money. . . .

WSJ: For novels such as "Blood Meridian," you did extensive historical research. What kind of research did you do for "The Road"?

CM: I don't know. Just talking to people about what things might look like under various catastrophic situations, but not a lot of research. I have these conversations on the phone with my brother Dennis, and quite often we get around to some sort of hideous end-of-the-world scenario and we always wind up just laughing. Anyone listening to this would say, "Why don't you just go home and get into a warm tub and open a vein." We talked about if there was a small percentage of the human population left, what would they do? They'd probably divide up into little tribes and when everything's gone, the only thing left to eat is each other. We know that's true historically.

WSJ: What does your brother Dennis do? Is he a scientist?

CM: He is. He has a doctorate in biology and he's also a lawyer and a thoughtful guy and a good friend.

WSJ: Brotherly conversation just turns to the apocalypse?

CM: More often than we can justify.

WSJ: What kind of reactions have you gotten to "The Road" from fathers?

CM: I have the same letter from about six different people. One from Australia, one from Germany, one from England, but they all said the same thing. They said, "I started reading your book after dinner and I finished it 3:45 the next morning, and I got up and went upstairs and I got my kids up and I just sat there in the bed and held them." . . .

WSJ: Is there a difference in the way humanity is portrayed in "The Road" as compared to "Blood Meridian"?

CM: There's not a lot of good guys in "Blood Meridian," whereas good guys is what "The Road" is about. That's the subject at hand.

John Hillcoat: I remember you said to me that "Blood Meridian" is about human evil, whereas "The Road" is about human goodness. It wasn't until I had my own son that I realized a personality was just innate in a person. You can see it forming. In "The Road," the boy has been born into a world where morals and ethics are out the window, almost like a science experiment. But he is the most moral character. Do you think people start as innately good?

CM: I don't think goodness is something that you learn. If you're left adrift in the world to learn goodness from it, you would be in trouble. But people tell me from time to time that my son John is just a wonderful kid. I tell people that he is so morally superior to me that I feel foolish correcting him about things, but I've got to do something—I'm his father. There's not much you can do to try to make a child into something that he's not. But whatever he is, you can sure destroy it. Just be mean and cruel and you can destroy the best person.

RUNE GRAULUND ON THE DESERT SETTING

McCarthy's fascination with the desert has been so strong that critics have been tempted to propose that McCarthy's very style is of the desert. McCarthy's prose, as the argument goes, is as spare as the desert landscape he describes, the texture of his writing as lean and stringent as his tone is sombre. These are arguably terms that can be tied to any sort of minimalist writing, yet to a writer whose authorship is based 'upon an intense awareness of impermanence [. . .] in a continual and more or less cordial dialogue with death' (Grammer 1999, 33), it does indeed seem 'as if the very hostility of this [desert] environment accommodated McCarthy's wilderness pastoralism better than any other setting' (Guillemin 2004, 75).

The following is first and foremost intended as an examination of the desert motif in *The Road* (2006), the latest of McCarthy's books. Strong as the desert motif may be from *Blood Meridian* on, it is of unprecedented importance in *The Road*; and this despite the fact that the word 'desert' appears but once in the text.[1] Physically, emotionally as morally, every choice the protagonists of *The Road* face as they trek across the bleak and abstract wasteland of a future America can in some way or other lead back to the ultimate question of *deserta*, of absence. The problem of the desert, in other words, is the barren ground upon which the central questions of the novel rest. . . .

. . . As the story of *The Road* opens, the reader is confronted by the two protagonists, a nameless man and his son, marooned in a world where both land and history have been decimated by an enigmatic cataclysm roughly a decade earlier. The landscape is in *The Road* an extreme of both presence and absence, more dominant than ever in McCarthy's authorship while paradoxically also the vaguest. Whether the landscapes in question are verdant and lush, like the fields and forests of *The Orchard Keeper* or *Outer Dark*, or naked, like the dry plains and mountains of *The Border Trilogy*, the landscapes described by McCarthy prior to *The Road* have always been vibrant, bustling with colour and energy, beautiful and moving even when cruel. Even in *Blood Meridian*, set in a landscape 'blasted and pitted by eons of natural violence—wind, water, earthquakes, volcanoes—into terrifying, sublime postures' (Owens 2000, 7) and easily the bleakest of McCarthy's books, the vistas described are always glorious. They may be frightening and overwhelming, but they are also magnificent, exciting and above all colourful, flaring shades of blue, yellow and green battling it out with an omnipresent red always 'the color of blood' (McCarthy 1990, 152).[3]

In comparison, the scenery of *The Road* is drab. In the place of stunning colours and extraordinary topography, a wall of grey greets the reader, a monochrome and 'wasted country' where all that moves is the 'ashes of the late world carried on the bleak and temporal winds to and fro in the void', an 'ashen scabland' where the only thing left 'rich in color' are dreams (McCarthy 2007, 4, 10, 14, 20). The landscape is so monotonous, so flat and so dull, that it does not really matter whether one moves or stays put. Unlike the journeys of John Grady Cole of *All the Pretty Horses* or Billy Parham of *The Crossing*, there is no possibility of a retreat to a world of simpler truths by going south of the border, no possibility of a return to a time of former innocence.[4] Instead, the characters of *The Road* are facing a landscape so vague it almost is not there, yet consequently also a landscape that comes to mean everything. There is nothing to cherish in the landscape, nothing to differentiate it from the next place down the road. Yet there is at the same time no denying it, simply because there is no escaping it.

* * *

As with place, so with time, for though history is still present in *The Road*, it is only as a fading memory. It is not a *totally* static world, yet it is one that obviously soon will be, a world in which time has stopped and a world in which progress and evolution are no longer to be found. It is thus a world entirely at the mercy of the Second Law of Thermodynamics (also known as the Law of Entropy), according to which 'the world acts spontaneously to minimize potentials', meaning that all energy will in time disperse and fizzle out. As the nameless man ponders near the conclusion of *The Road*, in a world governed by regression, this is the only real movement left: 'Perhaps in the world's destruction it would be possible at last to see how it was made. Oceans, mountains. The ponderous counterspectacle of things ceasing to be. The sweeping waste, hydroptic and coldly secular. The silence' (McCarthy 2007, 293). In the 'counterspectacle' of a world collapsing, all the prerequisites for history are necessarily fast disappearing. Nation states, machinery, books, social codes of civil conduct, even that basic ingredient of all advanced civilisations, the road, is breaking up:

> But there's not any more states?
> No.
> What happened to them?
> I don't know exactly. That's a good question.
> But the roads are still there.
> Yes. *For a while.*
> How long a while?
> I don't know. Maybe quite a while. There's nothing to uproot them so they should be okay for a while.
> (pp. 43–44, emphasis added)

The traces of humanity will linger on *for a while*, but as the nameless man knows all too well, traces are all that is left. In a world in which humanity is no longer humane, where survival is all and not even cannibalism and filicide are deemed unacceptable acts, all the man and his son can do is wait. There will be no tomorrow, no salvation from the encroaching nothingness that will in the end extinguish all that was once human.

As a post-apocalyptic vision of a future gone wrong, several of McCarthy's central topics are thus pre-empted from the outset by this uncharacteristic choice of setting. There is no longer a wild frontier to explore, no longer a bucolic respite to be gained from the complexities of modern life, simply because there is no longer a hinterland, no city and no civilisation against which the frontier and the rural can be measured. There are not even, as in *Blood Meridian*, any Indians left to scalp. Instead we find a desert that never ends nor begins, a landscape as devoid of difference as it is of life. . . .

. . . Contrary to all his former works, *The Road* is thus *not* a book that we can claim is 'unmistakeably and significantly from a specific region of the US' (Søfting 1999, 13).

There are, admittedly, as Chabon points out in his review, elements of the adventure story and the survival story, of man pitted against the environment and the bad guys down the road, elements that figure large in American literature and most certainly so in the tradition of the Western, the genre that McCarthy has to some extent or other operated within for the past twenty years. As Susan Kollin has pointed out, 'The Western landscape is supposed to be a test of character, bringing out the best in the hero and the worst in the villain' (Kollin 2001, 562), a trait turned on its head in the anti-Western of *Blood Meridian*, but one that fits *The Road* perfectly. The nameless man and his son continually reaffirm each other in the belief that they are 'the good guys', that they 'carry the fire' and that they will, in the end, triumph. In that sense, *The Road* could be read in terms of a prototypical Western, one whittled down to its pure essentials: a man and his boy, trying to make it across the frontier by fighting their way out of the claws of the bad guys, armed with just one gun but a set of morals firmer than that of any hero of the Old West.

This is in theory accurate, yet once again we must remember that the landscape faced by the man and the boy is not Western, not Southern, nor even a frontier of the most generic sorts.[6] Whether as a rejection of the heroic mythology of Manifest Destiny and endless expansion (*Blood Meridian*), or the nostalgic pining for a past defined by adventure and the unspoilt spectacular of a wilderness untouched by man (*The Border Trilogy*), *The Road* does not quite fit the bill. There is nothing 'adventurous' about the adventure of the nameless man and his son, nothing that is exciting in the sense of a Huck Finn waiting to see what thrilling experience may await round the next corner. Neither is there any real sense of nostalgia to be found, for although the nameless man obviously does not desire or cherish his atrocious circumstances, the realisation that he cannot afford sentimentalism—in any form or shape—forces him to squash out all remembrance of the past:

> He'd carried his billfold about till it wore a cornershaped hole in his trousers. Then one day he sat by the roadside and took it out and went through the contents. Some money, credit cards. His driver's licence. A picture of his wife. He spread everything out on the blacktop. Like gaming cards. He pitched the sweatblackened piece of leather into the woods and sat holding the photograph. Then he laid it down in the road also and then he stood and went on. (McCarthy 2007, 52–53)

Memories are a dangerous distraction from the one thing that truly matters: the present survival of his boy from one day to the other. As the novel progresses, the man becomes increasingly certain of what he has known all along, namely that whatever action he and his boy take, no matter how far they move, survival is not possible in the long run. And yet he keeps on moving, aware that there are no 'long term goals' (p. 170) but nevertheless forcing himself and his boy always to take one more step, hoping to locate one more meal before it all ends. 'Mostly he worried about their shoes. That and food. Always food' (p. 16). Temporally speaking, there is thus no real possibility to move either forwards or backwards, no chance for a return to the past nor any real hope for the future; all that is left is the immediate present, the next piece of bread, the next shelter, the next violent encounter that they have, somehow, to survive. In the hyper-pragmatic world the nameless man has wrought for himself and his son, the only way in which he can bear to go on living is to work with what he has at hand, however modest: 'So be it. Evoke the forms. Where you've nothing else construct ceremonies out of the air and breathe upon them' (pp. 77–78).

Precisely because of this incessant urgency to keep moving, the constant focus on the present or at most, the next day or week, neither the frontier nor that distinctly American nostalgia of 'being on the road' is particularly helpful categories to force onto *The Road*. Considering the title of the book, such a claim may sound absurd and self-contradictory, yet while it is true that the nameless man and his boy are constantly on the move, they are in fact not going anywhere. They are always 'on the road', but the point of being on the road rapidly dissolves into meaninglessness. In the beginning of the novel, we hear how the nameless man has decided they must go south since they cannot survive another winter. Yet as they eventually do make their way south and it becomes clear that their chances of survival have not improved, the futility of attempting to delineate differing categories (of any sorts) becomes painstakingly clear. One may move as much as one wants to, from north to south, from east to west, or vice versa; one may even move to the other side of the planet, to the shore across the grey ocean or plunge into its depths. But in the end it does not matter whether one moves or stays put. For in a world where everywhere is nowhere, a world in which there is no difference between frontier and civilisation, no difference between being on the road or off the road, everything eventually dissolves into meaninglessness and nothingness:

The world shrinking down about a raw core of parsible entities. The names of things slowly following those things into oblivion. Colors. The names of birds. Things to eat.

Finally the names of things one believed to be true. More
fragile than he would have thought. How much was gone
already? The sacred idiom shorn of its referents and so its
reality. Drawing down like something trying to preserve
heat. In time to wink out forever. (McCarthy 2007, 93)

Even the power of the word, McCarthy suggests, is in the end
divested of its power in the face of such devastation. In a world
'shrinking down', there can be no beyond, no redemption and
no hope. In such a world, there can be only desertion, a space
that is 'desert', bereft of any significance but the fact that it has
been forsaken.

* * *

George Monbiot of *The Guardian* has termed *The Road* 'the
most important environmental book ever written' (Monbiot
2007), a claim which may or may not prove to be true in terms
of its reception, but certainly a claim that becomes problematic
once authorial intent enters the equation. In a world in which
nature has been so decimated that it cannot rightly be said to
exist anymore, it is of course appropriate to question whether
the author has meant his book as a warning to a humanity
run rampant. The fact remains, however, that even the cataclysm, the event that so absolutely defines the terms of the
book's premise, remains ambiguous. The fundamental act of
anti-creation, the moment which in its destructiveness shaped
the world into its present form, even this is never disclosed in
enough detail for the reader to ascertain exactly what series of
events caused it. Critics like Monbiot have suggested the cataclysm to be caused by global warming, nuclear war, even the
strike of a meteor. But when studied closely, it is impossible to
say whether it is one or the other.

Since the man remembers a time distinctly unlike the one he
is living in, a time and a place where 'if he were God he would
have made the world just so and no different' (McCarthy 2007,
234), the change has obviously occurred relatively quickly,
possibly over the span of a few decades, years, months or even

seconds. Indeed, in one of the man's recollected memories, we are at one point told that, 'The clocks stopped at 1:17' (p. 54). The stopping of clocks followed by a 'long shear of light and then a series of low concussions' (p. 54) suggests that the cataclysm was sudden, yet beyond such scant information, we are told very little. Consequently, this scene *could* be read as the beginning of the end, a sudden and unforeseen event that the man will forever look back to as the point where the world he once knew first began to unravel. Yet McCarthy feeds us so little specific information that it is not possible to tell. As readers, we have no way of knowing whether the stopping of the clocks is but one more event in a string of similarly devastating but externally different events, one more memory of how the world was destroyed, but by no means the first.

In the present, as the man and the boy make their way from one charred and grey place to another more or less entirely like it, the readers are thus constantly face to face with the effects of the cataclysm, but the cause of these devastations is never entirely clear. Near the ending of the book, the man and the boy pass by a 'coastal city' with 'tall buildings vaguely askew [. . .] softened in the heat and reset again [. . .] melted window glass hung frozen down the walls like icing on a cake' (McCarthy 2007, 291). We are never told what might have caused such destruction, but neither are we meant to know. In *The Road*, rational causal explanations are largely useless simply because they are not supposed to make any rational sense as such. Except as a possible but by no means certain (and in all cases very imprecise) warning to protect and cherish the planet in its present state, politics do not provide a particularly useful approach to a reading of *The Road*. There is no real 'reason' for the cataclysmic event. There is simply its inescapable and massive presence.

In the post-historical and post-spatial world of *The Road*, all that remains is thus the relation between the coupling of man and boy, 'each the other's world entire' (McCarthy 2007, 4). Filed down to the bone, bereft of any distinguishing features, the external world offers nothing to the man and his boy other than an other against which they can define not just their own identities, but indeed their 'world entire'. Since '[t]here is no past' (p. 55), since '[t]here is no later' (p. 56), no people with whom they can identify and no place they can find peace, the man and the boy live in a constant present defined solely by the presence of their togetherness. As violence, cold and lack of food pose a constant threat to the survival of the unit that constitutes the man/boy coupling, the strangers they meet and the landscape they travel in are obviously of great significance; yet in the end, all of this is ultimately subordinated to the relationship between father and son.

Now Cormac McCarthy has never been willing to offer his readers the meaning of his books on a silver platter. As some of his critics have suggested, it may even be that the central meaning of McCarthy's authorship, the central message, is that there is no meaning to be found. In this sense, the desert seems the perfect setting, the ultimate scenery for a writer who seemingly adheres fully to Abbey's creed that the desert simply *is*: 'What does it mean? It means nothing. It is as it is and has no need for meaning' (Abbey 1971, 244). The all-consuming desert travelled by the man and his son means absolutely nothing but that it is omnipresent and that 'it is as it is'. This lack of meaning, then, must necessarily remain the central conundrum posed by *The Road*. Faced by surroundings of such complete meaninglessness, is it possible for any meaning to exist at all? Surprisingly, this is a question that McCarthy leaves suggestively, and optimistically, open.

* * *

Like all deserts, the landscape of *The Road* is one that is primarily characterised by absence: absence of sustenance, therefore of life, hence ultimately of presence. Deriving from Latin *desertus* meaning 'abandoned, deserted, left' (*Oxford English Dictionary*), the desert is etymologically defined by negation, hence delineated by what it is *not* rather than what it *is*. One thing that is present in the desert, however, is death. As Charles

Bowden remarks in *Blue Desert* (1986), in a landscape otherwise devoid of defining characteristics, death becomes its defining state, the one concept summing up a landscape otherwise so hard to summarise:

> I have no simple handle on the desert. Murder, rape, robbery, capital punishment, high interest, the stock market—all these matters produce quick and easy opinions. But not the hot, dry ground. I have walked hundreds and hundreds and hundreds of miles in the desert and yet my thoughts about it are very few and I spend very little time thinking these thoughts. [Yet] here I know this fact: the desert is where I want to die, where I do not fear death, do not even consider it. Here death is like breathing. Here death simply is. (Bowden 1997, 143)

Desert travellers (literary as actual) seeking death are thus a common enough phenomenon, for in a landscape as void as the desert, there is often very little other reason to go there. Precisely because travellers like Bowden have *chosen* to engage with death, they can, however, also afford to be cavalier about it.

The problem of all wildernesses, and in particular wildernesses as impoverished as those of the desert, is that if death is forced upon you, if you find yourself in a space where death is indeed 'like breathing' (Bowden), the charm of dying wears off rather quickly. This is precisely the problem faced by the man and the boy as they find themselves in a space where they have to 'inhale' death every year, every day and every hour, a presence they have as little hope of escaping as the necessity to take another breath. Consequently, they find themselves in a state in which it is very difficult to appreciate anything, even survival itself. The proximity of death may be exciting as well as beautiful, yet as Edmund Burke and Immanuel Kant remarked in their studies of the sublime, there is nothing exhilarating about death when it comes *too* close. . . .

. . . It is thus another and far less celebrated 'desert truth' that *The Road* affirms, namely that in a landscape in which death reigns supreme, it is impossible to uphold romantic illusions of beauty, truth, honour, compassion or any other lofty sentiments. Unlike Abbey who sees the 'finest quality' of the desert to be its 'indifference [. . .] to our presence, our absence, our coming, our staying or our going' simply because of his belief that no matter what happens, 'living things will emerge' (Abbey 1971, 334), even comforts like these are denied in a world that is as truly and absolutely deserted as that of *The Road*. In the face of relentless pressure from such universal devastation, neither life nor truth can sustain a foothold in the long run. The man stoically attempts to keep 'little truths' alive, the hope of another meal, warmth, a place to sleep, and most essentially, the hope that truth and survival somehow matter. The further he and his son progress into nothingness, however, the more hopeless their situation becomes, the man is eventually forced to admit that even the simple truth of survival itself eventually withers. In a world where nothing new ever comes forth, a world in which the possibility of growth and regeneration is void, the man realises that even just to go on living is to live a life where, 'Every day is a lie' (McCarthy 2007, 254). Hence, in a world in which there cannot be survival in even the basest of its forms, there can as consequence be no truths or lies, no right or wrong, no morals or ethics, no bad guys or good guys. In a fading world like this, a world 'shadowless and without feature' (p. 189), the one and only 'absolute truth' (p. 138) remains that: 'you are dying. That is not a lie' (p. 254).

* * *

As it turns out, however, the man may be wrong in this assumption. For contrary to all that McCarthy has ever taught his readers to expect, contrary to his partiality for dire endings, and most certainly contrary to the preceding three hundred pages of the novel, the concluding ten pages of *The Road* grant us a highly surprising finale: an ending that, while not exactly happy, at least contains the seeds for a new beginning.

'Can you do it? When the time comes? Can you?' (McCarthy 2007, 28), the man asks himself in the beginning of the book, a question that is at the end answered in the negative as he realises that, 'I cant hold my son dead in my arms' (p. 298). The man dies but is not able to fulfil his grim pledge. The ever dwindling spiral of hope that has throughout the novel plummeted deeper and deeper does not, after all, crash and burn. 'You dont know what might be down the road' (p. 297), the dying father admonishes his son, thus contradicting the earlier despairing insight that death remains the one and only real truth we can ever count on.

McCarthy could have stopped the book here and there would have been no marked break from form. This fresh spark of hope in the dark, a spark that once more relights 'the fire' that the man and his son have tried so hard throughout to maintain, could have been left a flickering and unsteady glow that the boy was left to carry, alone, out of the reader's sight. For once, however, McCarthy seems unwilling, incapable even, of such cynicism. Introducing a *deus ex machina* worthy of Euripides, the good guys magically manifest themselves almost instantly the father dies, consequently validating the father's words in physical as well as conceptual form. Contrary to all former expectations, it turns out that good guys *do exist*, in essence as in presence. Not only is the boy rewarded for his persistence in trying to be good, confirmed in the belief that *it does matter* to be good. He is also shown that goodness is able to exist outside the close-knit union of father and son, hence that the world outside the father–son relationship, formerly 'the world entire', is still invested with meaning, purpose and future. Taken in by kindred spirits, a man and a woman, a little boy and a little girl, it seems the world may not be dying after all. Hope, otherwise in short supply in McCarthy's authorship and never before living under tougher conditions than in *The Road*, is suddenly present in abundance.

* * *

So what, exactly, are we to believe of that central question posed by the book's desert premise?

If we momentarily ignore both the boy and the ending, the answer to this question seems to be that survival is the one concern that rules out all others. As the man sums it up at the end: 'A lot of bad things have happened but we're still here. [. . .] It counts for something' (McCarthy 2007, 287, 288). It is vital for the basic truth of life itself to be secured before the more refined truths of ethics and aesthetics have any chance to develop and grow. To put it crudely, the set of rules by which the man lives, the one truth that rules out all other truths, boils down to a simple credo of 'survive first, ask questions later'.

This equation of course becomes far more complicated when we add the boy's concerns. To the boy, base survival is not enough. The boy needs to invest life with meaning beyond the simple mechanics of continued survival. This need manifests itself in many different ways, but most explicitly so in his horror of cannibalism. In a world largely 'populated by men who would eat your children in front of your eyes' (McCarthy 2007, 192), it is imperative for the boy that he and his father do not themselves stoop to this level. The boy can to some degree accept his father's minor moral failings—his lack of compassion towards strangers, his occasional lapses of honesty—but makes it clear that cannibalism is the one sin he will never be able to forgive. Again and again, the boy asks the man for reassurance that they will not transgress this fundamental boundary no matter how desperate they may become. This promise the man continually reaffirms.

Given his constant need for affirmation, however, it seems likely that the boy suspects the same as the reader, namely that the man would be able to transgress not just this prohibition, but any, as long as it serves that central premise of keeping his boy alive. As much as the man marvels and wonders at the boy's immense capacity for 'goodness', the boy's insistence on moral rectitude remains a quality that inevitably puts man and boy at cross-purposes. For the man, all other concerns are subsumed under the umbrella of survival. He will not allow the few non-violent strangers they meet on their way entry into their companionship, nor will he even temporarily share their food and shelter. From the man's point of view, any one such act of compassion, no matter how small, will constitute an unpardonable lowering of his guard, directly as indirectly; most immediately so through the possibility of physical assault, but possibly even more so in a lessening of their long-term chances through the squandering away of their already meagre resources. As the man is painfully aware, however, for every refusal of help, the boy becomes further and further removed, not just from the man but also from himself, to the point that 'something was gone that could not be put right again' (McCarthy 2007, 145).

As a consequence of this realisation, the man is against his better judgement occasionally forced to depart from his strict survival regimen. Limited kindnesses are now and again extended to strangers, just as the boy is twice allowed to bathe (first in a pool, later in the ocean) for no other reason than because he wants to. Nowhere better is this dilemma of survival versus good summed up, however, than when the man discovers a flare gun. As father and son ponder the potential uses of the gun, the man admits he does not plan to use it as it was originally intended since 'there's nobody to signal to' (McCarthy 2007, 258). Instead, he aims to use it as a weapon. To this, the boy asks whether they can fire it for 'celebration' (p. 258) rather than harm. According to the man's no-nonsense code of survival, firing the gun will be a pointless gesture, one that will not just waste ammunition but might also alert the roaming bad guys to their presence. Accordingly, firing the gun for 'celebration' may in one way or another be the cause of their death and it should, from a survivalist point of view, remain unfired. As the man also realises, however, if he does not allow his son to fire the gun, the outcome may in the long run be equally fatal. Forever barring his son from any 'celebration', from wonder, it is painfully clear to the man that the boy will eventually not even be able to celebrate that greatest wonder of all, that of life itself.

* * *

In terms of its central desert premise, the conclusion of *The Road* must necessarily therefore be two-pronged.

On one hand it is a novel that is squarely anthropocentric, arguing that since humanity is the only source (and interpreter) of meaning, ethics and beauty, human survival takes precedence over all else. It is not the case of human survival as a species, but that specific part of the human species capable of 'humanity', or in the terms of man and the boy, of 'goodness'. Wilderness, nature, beasts or beastmen, the survival of all such is of no significance as long as 'the good guys' survive. A lesson in anthropocentrism that not only becomes reinforced in the light of the ending, but seems to suggest that a humanist belief in the tenet of goodness is not only worth more than the remainder of creation, but actually able to sustain itself independently of it. In other words, it is not solely a question of realising that the survival of those who 'carry the fire' takes precedence over that of all other living things, but also that the 'fire' (goodness) seems able to generate heat even when no fuel is present. Sunlight and food, clean water and all that grows may cease to exist, yet innocence and goodness never will: 'Goodness will find the little boy. It always has. It will again' (McCarthy 2007, 300).

On the other hand, the second and contradictory desert lesson to be learned from *The Road* is that without nature, without a 'biosphere' (Monbiot 2007), there can be no humanity either, hence that for 'goodness' to take seed and grow, rich and fertile soil is an absolute prerequisite. Human will and intention may be the very finest, but in a world that is *total* desert, humanity cannot prevail, no matter how hopeful, good, innocent or moral. For where would it go? The good guys magically appearing at the end of *The Road* must necessarily come from *somewhere*, just as their continued survival must imply that the desert is not quite as total as the man, the son and we as readers have hitherto been led to believe.

* * *

While we cannot with any certainty say whether it is one or the other, it is, however, remarkable just how ardently McCarthy seems to need to *believe* the latter. Which brings us to a subject that we have so far been careful to stay clear of, a third character that may be as important as the man and the boy although he is conspicuously absent throughout.

As Edwin T. Arnold has suggested, although McCarthy can easily be taken for a nihilist, 'there is also evident in his work a profound belief in the need for moral order, a conviction that is essentially religious' (Arnold 1999, 46). This need for a moral order has never been clearer in McCarthy's authorship than in *The Road*. The man again and again addresses God, though mostly in curses: 'Are you there? he whispered. Will I see you at the last? Have you a neck by which to throttle you? Have you a heart? Damn you eternally have you a soul? Oh God, he whispered. Oh God' (McCarthy 2007, 10). Angry as he is at this absent God, it is obvious that the man is no atheist. The man, who is the very essence of fatherhood, passionately needs to believe in the existence of God, the absent Father. First of all because this would open the possibility of apportioning blame and hence enact causality and meaning once more (the apocalypse happened because God has willed it/has failed), but most of all because this means an entertaining of the hope that the absent father might at one point return in order to restore the world and relieve the man of his burden. Since God refuses to manifest, however, the hope invested in divinity is eventually transferred to the one being that quite literally seems to be of another, and future, world. Meeting an old man whose name may or may not be Ely, the man suggests that since 'There is no God' (p. 181), perhaps instead the boy is 'a god' (p. 183).[7] Not God, capital G, but *a* god, a prophet of the world to come once the leftovers of the old world have been laid to rest, a spark of life that will enable creation to begin anew.

Once again, however, we just cannot tell. As the man at one point ponders the solitary flute-playing of his son, so are we as readers left to wonder whether such optimism of a new beginning represents: 'A formless music for the age to come. Or perhaps the last music on earth called up from out of the ashes of its ruin' (McCarthy 2007, 81). Insofar as the unexpected ending could be constructed as divine intervention and proof of God's will on earth, or, failing that, that the goodness of the boy constitutes a law unto itself that will form a new divinity, we are, at the very end, left wondering, as uncertain as ever.

* * *

What remains amidst all this indecisiveness, however, is a strong core of hope and it is on this bedrock that McCarthy makes his final stand. Depending on what one comes looking for, *The Road* can convincingly sustain readings that suggest we invest our hopes *either* in nature, in humanity or in God. As has hopefully been proved here, any reading focusing solely on one interpretation will have to ignore quite a few signs to the contrary in a novel that tellingly ends with the word 'mystery' (McCarthy 2007, 307).[8] Wherever one decides to put one's stake, there can hardly be any doubt, though, that *The Road* expresses a passionate hope that *hope itself* matters. Even if it does not absolutely confirm that hope leads to redemption, even if we do not get any definite answers one way or the other, at least *The Road* opens up the possibility that hope *might* matter. 'This is what the good guys do. They keep trying. They don't give up' (p. 145).

Notes

1. The one time the word 'desert' appears in the text, it is in the sense of 'dessert', that is, of food: 'They ate little mushrooms together with the beans and drank tea and had tinned pears for their dessert' (McCarthy 2007, 41).

3. For one particularly good passage of landscape in colour (mainly various shades of blue and red), see chapter 4 of *Blood Meridian*. For a discussion of the symbolism of colour in McCarthy more generally and in particular of *Cities on the Plain*, see Owens 2000, chap. 5.

4. 'Mexico becomes a region where the hero from the north of the border loses his bearing and his sense of identity', a place 'wholly alien and wholly strange' (Kollin 2001, 580). Also, 'In a book that is part of a "Border Trilogy," one of the central themes of which is the vast differences between our two countries, there is significance in the implication that even the weather recognizes that border' (Campbell 2002, 47).

6. For a frontier (a zone of transition) to exist, after all, one needs something to differentiate it from: a region that is civilised as well as a space that is barbaric.

7. The symbolism is hard to miss here since 'Eli' in Aramaic of course means 'my God'.

8. The final half page of the book manages once again to abort the cautious note of anthropocentric optimism offered by the boy's redemption by insisting that there is in the world 'a thing which could not be put back. Not be made right again'. The very final conclusion to the book is thus simultaneously ominous, to some extent undermining the sense of closure of the boy's salvation from evil, while at the same time oddly if hesitantly celebratory, cherishing the 'mystery' of 'all things [. . .] older than man' (McCarthy 2007, 307).

Bibliography

Abbey, E. 1971, *Desert Solitaire: A Season in the Wilderness*, Ballantine Books, New York.

Arnold, E. T. 1999, 'Naming, knowing and nothingness: McCarthy's moral parables' in *Perspectives on Cormac McCarthy*, ed. E. T. Arnold & D. Luce, University Press of Mississippi, Jackson, Miss., pp. 221–247.

Bowden, C. 1997, *Blue Desert*, University of Arizona Press, Tucson, Ariz.

Burke, E. 1990, *A Philosophical Enquiry*, Oxford University Press, Oxford & New York.

Campbell, C. D. 2002, 'Walter de Maria's lightning field and McCarthy's enigmatic epilogue: "Y qué clase de lugar es éste?"' *The Cormac McCarthy Journal*, vol. 2, Spring, pp. 40–55.

Chabon, M. 2007, 'After the apocalypse', *The New York Review of Books*, vol. 54, no. 2, at http://www.nybooks.com/articles/19856 (accessed 5 Oct. 2009).

Daugherty, L. 1999, '"The very life of the darkness": *Blood Meridian* as gnostic tragedy' in *Perspectives on Cormac McCarthy*, ed. E. T. Arnold & D. Luce, University Press of Mississippi, Jackson, Miss., pp. 159–174.

Grammer, J. M. 1999, 'A thing against which time will not prevail: Pastoral and history in Cormac McCarthy's South' in *Perspectives on Cormac McCarthy*, ed. E. T. Arnold & D. Luce, University Press of Mississippi, Jackson, Miss., pp. 29–44.

Guillemin, G. 2004, *The Pastoral Vision of Cormac McCarthy*, Texas A&M Press, College Station, Tex.

Kant, I. 1992, 'Analytic of the sublime' in Critique of Judgment [1790], in *Critical Theory Since Plato—Revised Edition*, ed. H. Adams, Harcourt Brace, New York.

Kollin, S. 2001, 'Genre and the geographies of violence: Cormac McCarthy and the contemporary Western', *Contemporary Literature*, vol. 42, no. 3, pp. 557–588.

McCarthy, C. 1990, *Blood Meridian, or, The Evening Redness in the West*, Picador, Basingstoke & Oxford.

McCarthy, C. 2007, *The Road*, Picador, Basingstoke & Oxford.

Monbiot, G. 2007, 'Civilisation ends with a shutdown of human concern. Are we there already?' *The Guardian*, 30 Oct., at shttp://www.guardian.co.uk/commentisfree/2007/oct/30/comment.books (accessed 5 Oct. 2009).

Owens, B. 2000, *Cormac McCarthy's Western Novels*, University of Arizona Press, Tucson, Ariz.

Phillips, D. 1996, 'History and the ugly facts of Cormac McCarthy's *Blood Meridian*', *American Literature*, vol. 68, June, pp. 433–460.

Sepich, J. E. 1999, '"What kind of Indians was them?": Some historical sources in Cormac McCarthy's *Blood Meridian*' in *Perspectives on Cormac McCarthy*, ed. E. T. Arnold & D. Luce, University Press of Mississippi, Jackson, Miss. pp. 123–144.

Shaviro, S. 1999, 'A reading of *Blood Meridian*' in *Perspectives on Cormac McCarthy*, ed. E. T. Arnold & D. Luce, University Press of Mississippi, Jackson, Miss., pp. 145–158.

Slovic, S. 2001, 'Introduction' in *Getting Over the Color Green: Contemporary Environmental Literature of the Southwest*, ed. S. Slovic, University of Arizona Press, Tucson, Ariz.

Søfting, I. A. 1999, 'Desert pandemonium: Cormac McCarthy's apocalyptic "Western" in *Blood Meridian*', *American Studies in Scandinavia*, vol. 31, pp. 13–30.

Works by Cormac McCarthy

Novels

The Orchard Keeper, 1965.

Outer Dark, 1968.

Child of God, 1974.

Suttree, 1979.

Blood Meridian, Or the Evening Redness in the West, 1985.

All the Pretty Horses, 1992.

The Crossing, 1994.

Cities of the Plain, 1998.

No Country for Old Men, 2005.

The Road, 2006.

Plays and Screenplays

The Stonemason: A Play in Five Acts, 1994.

The Gardener's Son: A Screenplay, 1996.

The Sunset Limited: A Novel in Dramatic Form, 2006.

Annotated Bibliography

Bennett, Barbara. "Celtic Influences on Cormac McCarthy's *No Country for Old Men* and *The Road.*" *Notes on Contemporary Literature* 38.5 (2008): 2–3.

The author traces the Celtic influences and allusions found in McCarthy's most recent novels. In particular, she identifies and analyzes the centrality of the hearth fire and McCarthy's direct and indirect citations of the poetry of William Butler Yeats.

Bloom, Harold. Interview with Leonard Pierce. *A.V. Club.* 15 June 2009. <http://www.avclub.com/articles/harold-bloom-on-blood-meridian,29214/>

In this online interview, renowned literary critic Harold Bloom discusses Cormac McCarthy's earlier masterpiece, *Blood Meridian.* Though he mentions *The Road* only briefly, many of Bloom's points about the previous novel's thematic concerns with violence and the existence of God offer important insights into *The Road* and help locate the novel in the context of McCarthy's literary career.

Cant, John. "*The Road.*" *Cormac McCarthy*, Bloom's Modern Critical Views. New York: Chelsea House, 2008, pp. 183–200.

The author views the novel as a return to the rich, poetic rhetoric that distinguished *Suttree* and *Blood Meridian.* The work is also presented as a reengagement on McCarthy's part of fundamental philosophical questions that influence *The Road's* structure and formal elements.

Carlson, Thomas A. "With the World at Heart: Reading Cormac McCarthy's *The Road* with Augustine and Heidegger." *Religion & Literature* 39.3 (2007): 47–71.

In this philosophically challenging but rich and engaging essay, the author uses the writings of the early Christian thinker St. Augustine and of the twentieth-century philosopher Martin Heidegger to elucidate the experience of loss and nothingness in *The*

Road. For Carlson, the extreme deprivations faced by the characters in *The Road* reveal the essence of existence, including the certainty of love and the real possibility of the existence of God.

Chabon, Michael. "Dark Adventure: On Cormac McCarthy's *The Road.*" *Maps and Legends: Reading and Writing along the Borderlands.* San Francisco: McSweeney's Books, 2008, pp. 107–20.

In this essay, novelist Michael Chabon discusses the genre conventions at work in *The Road.* While Chabon claims that the novel demonstrates elements of postapocalyptic fiction, modern adventure stories, and the classical epic, he finds it fits best within the tradition of the gothic horror story, with its emphasis on nightmare and human depravity and its exposure of deep-seated fears (in this case, the fears and anxieties parents feel for their children).

Graulund, Rune. "Fulcrums and Borderlands: A Desert Reading of Cormac McCarthy's *The Road.*" *Orbis Litterarum* 65.1 (2010): 57–78.

This article explores the setting and imagery of the desert as a recurring motif in McCarthy's fiction, tracing its roots in the bleak expanses of *Blood Meridian.* Graulund equates the wanderings of the father and son across the bleak and abstract landscape of *The Road* with a journey to absence and self-negation.

Grindley, Carl James. "The Setting of McCarthy's *The Road.*" *The Explicator* 67.1 (2008): 11–13.

In this brief essay, the author discusses the North American setting of *The Road*, arguing that the postapocalyptic landscape is, in fact, post apocalypse; that is, the world after the final judgment has separated the blessed and the damned.

Hunt, Alex, and Martin M. Jacobsen. "Cormac McCarthy's *The Road* and Plato's Simile of the Sun." *The Explicator* 66.3 (2008): 155–58.

The authors discuss McCarthy's allusions to classical tropes equating light and the sun with wisdom, truth, and hope. The novel's light and dark imagery references Plato's *Republic*, in particular the Simile of the Sun and the Allegory of the Cave. The authors suggest that McCarthy revises Plato's allegory, making the power and fragility of language, and the ways language enables meaning and civilization, a central theme in his novel.

Jurgensen, John. "Hollywood's Favorite Cowboy." *Wall Street Journal*, November 20, 2009.

This interview reveals the backstory behind *The Road*, as well as McCarthy's views on the novel's treatment of God, on the importance of the father-son bond, and on whether goodness is inherent in an individual or learned.

Kunsa, Ashley. "'Maps of the World in Its Becoming': Post-Apocalyptic Naming in Cormac McCarthy's *The Road*." *Journal of Modern Literature* 33.1 (2009): 57–74.

Kunsa argues that the spare language of *The Road* is key to understanding the journey as a motif in the novel. The language of the novel enables a journey from ironic nihilism to an optimistic worldview and argues for a return to the core elements of narrative.

Rambo, Shelly L. "Beyond Redemption?: Reading Cormac McCarthy's *The Road* after the End of the World." *Studies in the Literary Imagination* 41.2 (2008): 99–120.

This scholarly article addresses redemption in *The Road*. Rambo discusses redemption as a recurrent theme in American literature as a whole, and she argues that *The Road* employs the language of redemption in order to suggest its irrevocable loss in this new and violent world. Rambo's argument contrasts significantly with the more popular evaluation of the novel as a redemptive and ultimately uplifting work.

Schaub, Thomas H. "Secular Scripture and Cormac McCarthy's *The Road*." *Renascence* 61.3 (2009): 153–67.

In this thoroughly researched essay, Schaub discusses *The Road* as a richly literary work concerned with how spiritual belief might survive in a world void of God, a purely secular realm.

He explores the layers of allusion in *The Road*, discussing the influence of such writers as Dante, Ernest Hemingway, and Flannery O'Connor, while offering many salient descriptions of McCarthy's style and its relation to the novel's themes. If the novel seems to nullify meaning and divinity, Schaub argues, the father's efforts at storytelling (and the novel itself) restore reality for both the son and the reader.

Shy, Todd. Review of *The Road*. *The Christian Century*, March 6, 2007: 38–41.

This review helps place the novel in a religious context by identifying its strong connection to the biblical book of Job, which is a theodicy or explanation of the existence of evil.

Contributors

Harold Bloom is Sterling Professor of the Humanities at Yale University. Educated at Cornell and Yale universities, he is the author of more than 30 books, including *Shelley's Mythmaking* (1959), *Blake's Apocalypse* (1963), *Yeats* (1970), *The Anxiety of Influence* (1973), *A Map of Misreading* (1975), *Kabbalah and Criticism* (1975), *Agon: Toward a Theory of Revisionism* (1982), *The American Religion* (1992), *The Western Canon* (1994), *Omens of Millennium: The Gnosis of Angels, Dreams, and Resurrection* (1996), *Shakespeare: The Invention of the Human* (1998), *How to Read and Why* (2000), *Genius: A Mosaic of One Hundred Exemplary Creative Minds* (2002), *Hamlet: Poem Unlimited* (2003), *Where Shall Wisdom Be Found?* (2004), *Jesus and Yahweh: The Names Divine* (2005), and *Till I End My Song: A Gathering of Last Poems* (2010). In addition, he is the author of hundreds of articles, reviews, and editorial introductions. In 1999, Professor Bloom received the American Academy of Arts and Letters' Gold Medal for Criticism. He has also received the International Prize of Catalonia, the Alfonso Reyes Prize of Mexico, and the Hans Christian Andersen Bicentennial Prize of Denmark.

Todd Shy is a writer based in Raleigh, North Carolina. He is a regular contributor to the Raleigh *News & Observer* and teaches at Cary Academy.

Thomas A. Carlson is an associate professor in the department of religious studies at the University of California at Santa Barbara. He is the author of *Indiscretion: Finitude and the Naming of God* (1999) and *The Indiscrete Image: Infinitude and Creation of the Human* (2008). His article on *The Road* was presented as the 2007 Religion and Literature lecture at the University of Notre Dame.

Carl James Grindley is consortial associate professor of communications and culture in the Online Baccalaureate Program of the City University of New York's School of

Professional Studies and director of college honors programs, director of instructional technology, and associate professor of English at Eugenio María de Hostos Community College, also at the City University of New York.

Alex Hunt is associate professor of English at West Texas A&M University.

Martin M. Jacobsen is associate professor of English at West Texas A&M University, where he teaches composition, literature, and linguistics classes. He is the author of *Transformations of Literacy in Computer-Mediated Communication: Orality, Literacy, Cyberdiscursivity* (2002). His research interests include discourse analysis and rhetorical theory.

Barbara Bennett is a professor of literature at North Carolina State University. She is the author of *Comic Visions, Female Voices: Contemporary Women Novelists and Southern Humor* (1998), *Understanding Jill McCorkle* (2000), and *Soul of a Lion: One Woman's Quest to Save Africa's Wildlife Refugees* (2010).

Shelly Rambo is assistant professor of theology at Boston University School of Theology. Her research and teaching interests focus on religious responses to suffering, trauma, and violence, and she is the author of *Trauma and Redemption: Witnessing Spirit Between Death and Life* (2010).

Ashley Kunsa has taught at Penn State University and is currently an instructor at West Virginia University.

John Jurgensen writes for the *Wall Street Journal*. Previously he reported for *The Hartford Courant* and the Associated Press.

Rune Graulund received a Ph.D. from Goldsmith College in London and has taught at the University of London and the University of Copenhagen. He has published on postcolonial writing, travel writing, and contemporary American fiction and is the editor of *Postcolonial Travel Writing*.

Acknowledgments

Todd Shy, "The Road." From *Christian Century*, March 6, 2007: 38–41. Copyright © 2007 *Christian Century*.

Thomas A. Carlson, "With the World at Heart: Reading Cormac McCarthy's *The Road* with Augustine and Heidegger." From *Religion & Literature* 39, no. 3 (Autumn 2007): 54–62. Copyright © 2007 *Religion & Literature*.

Carl James Grindley, "The Setting of McCarthy's *The Road*." From *The Explicator* 67, no. 1 (2008): 11–13. Copyright © 2008 *The Explicator*.

Alex Hunt and Martin M. Jacobsen, "Cormac McCarthy's *The Road* and Plato's Simile of the Sun." From *The Explicator* 66, no. 3 (2008): 155–58. Copyright © 2008 *The Explicator*.

Barbara Bennett, "Celtic Influences on Cormac McCarthy's *No Country for Old Men* and *The Road*." From *Notes on Contemporary Literature* 38, no. 5 (2008): 2–3. Copyright © 2008 by William S. Doxey.

Shelly L. Rambo, "Beyond Redemption? Reading *The Road* at the End of the World" was originally published in *Studies in the Literary Imagination* 41, no. 2 (Fall 2008): 99–120. Copyright © 2008, Georgia State University. Reproduced by permission.

Ashley Kunsa, "'Maps of the World in Its Becoming': Post-Apocalyptic Naming in Cormac McCarthy's *The Road*." From *Journal of Modern Literature* 33, no. 1 (2009): 57–74.

John Jurgensen, "Hollywood's Favorite Cowboy." From *The Wall Street Journal*, November 13, 2009, p. W-1. Copyright © 2009 Dow Jones and Company.

Rune Grauland, "Fulcrums and Borderlands: A Desert Reading of Cormac McCarthy's *The Road*." From *Orbis Literatum* 65, no. 1 (2010): 57–78. Copyright © 2010 Blackwell Publishing.

Index